MAC DRE

"Simply Amazing" – Author Skyla Torres

the LIFE *and* TIMES *of*

KING GURU

Copyright © 2024 Wilberto Belardo.

All rights reserved. This book or any portion thereof may not be reproduced or used in any manner whatsoever without the express written permission of the publisher except for the use of brief quotations in a book review.

Printed by KG Enterprise,
in the United States of America.

First printing, 2024.

Cover image by King Guru.

KG Enterprise
PO Box 800412
Houston, Texas, 77055

AUTHOR'S NOTE

I want to start this off by saying R.I.P. Mac Dre! Mac Dre was a legendary rapper who I personally grew up listening to. I loved his music just as much as all his fans did and I hope I did his memory justice by bringing his story to life.

It really wasn't that hard for me to write this book because Mac Dre's life was so interesting that all I had to do was tell his story. So, although I may have added scenes for dramatic purposes I can wholeheartedly say this story is basically what really took place.

I really appreciate all my fans (new and old). Rest assured that this is an authentic King Guru production. So if you opened this book hoping to hop in the passenger seat of the car the narrator is driving in, trust and believe that's exactly what's about to take place.

With that being said, let's get this journey started…

King Guru

CONTENTS

Chapter One 1

Chapter Two 11

Chapter Three 22

Chapter Four 33

Chapter Five 43

Chapter Six 55

Chapter Seven 65

Chapter Eight 74

Chapter Nine 81

Chapter Ten 93

Chapter Eleven 105

Chapter Twelve 108

Chapter Thirteen 114

Chapter Fourteen 122

Chapter Fifteen 129

Chapter Sixteen 137

Chapter Seventeen 144

Chapter Eighteen 155

Chapter Nineteen 163

Chapter Twenty 171

Chapter Twenty One.. 176

Chapter Twenty Two 182

Chapter Twenty Three... 188

Chapter Twenty Four.. 191

Chapter Twenty Five... 198

Chapter Twenty Six... 205

Chapter Twenty Seven 213

Chapter Twenty Eight... 225

Chapter Twenty Nine.. 231

Chapter Thirty.. 240

Chapter Thirty One... 246

Chapter Thirty Two.. 259

Chapter Thirty Three.. 267

Chapter Thirty Four.. 275

CHAPTER ONE

"Once upon a time, before I had CD, I was on the block with rocks and hella bags of weed."
- Mac Dre

Welcome to an official Stomp-Out Committee convention. I'm Mac Dre, and I'm gonna be your guide through the realest story ever told.

If you're into Bay Area Hyphy music, you already know who I am. Or, better yet, who I was before I died. I was born in Oakland, California. My momma named me Andre so everybody called me Dre. I put the "Mac" in front of my name after the cuddy, The Mac. The Mac was a real North Pole nigga who lost his life way too early. But, I'll get into all'at a little later.

Before I move on, I do gotta say this: Mac isn't just a fly sounding name. M.A.C. is an acronym for Master AT Communicating. In the Bay, your mouthpiece can get you into backrooms and board rooms.

Therefore, your communication gotta be up to par on every level. As far as my u-n-I-verses go, my words are slicker than baby oil.

For the record, I'm not a rapper who created a persona of a player, pimp or gangsta. For me, it was the other way around. I'm just like any other nigga who came up in the ghetto. I experienced every level of the game from selling rocks to bustin' choppers. I started out as a young juvenile delinquent and made it to the upper echelons of the music industry. And, this is my story...

A lot of people use the term *jump off the porch*, when they speak about the time in their life when they were introduced to the streets or the game. For me, it was different. I never sought out the streets because I was born into it. I was a wild-ass Bebe's kid born in the ghetto to a single mother who did the best she could with the tools that were given to her.

Moms' was a beautiful Black woman who loved to party. I can't remember a time when she didn't have a house full people smoking and drinking while the music cultivated the mood.

We moved around a lot when I was little. But, momma eventually got Section 8 and we got a small house in a Vallejo neighborhood called Country Club Crest. The Crest has several names, tho'; 3 C's, North Pole, or The Crestside.

The Crest is a neighborhood that mostly consist of single family homes. We don't have high-rise apartment buildings or low income housing projects. But, it is a ghetto on the Northside of Vallejo. Since the houses are all older, and all the white folks moved away, the rent was cheap. Thus, making it a ghetto.

Vallejo is just like any other city in the Bay Area. It's fast and multicultural. It's a beautiful place with a dark history. Since I came up in the 80's, I gotta give it to you from my perspective of that era.

I'ma give it to you raw. The Bay Area was the epicenter of the crack epidemic while I was growing up and that's why some people refer to it as the "Yea Area." I'm not gonna take anything away from L.A. They had real bosses like Harry O and Freeway Rick Ross. They did they shit. But Little D had the Bay turnt' up!

When you think of the Bay, you need to keep in mind it sits on water. The Pacific Ocean is right there. But, we don't got sunny beaches with tanned peaches getting displayed on the sand. We got docks and railroad cars moving products that arrive on big boats from far away places like China, Columbia and Central America. For sophisticated crime syndicates who traffic in products like powder and pistols, the Bay is a major distribution hub. Add in the fact that Oakland, Frisco, Richmond and Vallejo are melting pots for poor minorities and you've got a perfect storm.

I'm not saying the drug epidemic of the 80's is what turnt' up Northern Cali. The flood of cocaine did turn the streets upside down, but the counter culture was always there. The Bay was the home of the Black Panthers. Further into the valley, in Sacramento, was where a group of strapped Panthers entered the State Capital on some real gangsta shit. We always had strong, intelligent Black men pushing lines in the Bay.

When cocaine came, the energy it emitted flooded our waterways with sex, money and murder. It turnt' the back alleys into front streets. It was as if the sun's rays were blocked by crack smoke...

In my neighborhood, everyone's moms' and pops' were hooked on rocks. Technically, none of my cuddies had fathers around, but that's neither here nor there. Either way, everyone seemed to be smoked out around my, so it really didn't matter if you had both parents, or not. It wasn't like anyone was really watching us, anyway. Even if they were watching us, there wasn't much guidance, so it really wouldn't have mattered much.

Regardless of the era, and what was going on in the world, I love my life and wouldn't change anything about my childhood. If anything, I'd probably change a thing or two about how I moved the night I died. But that's a whole 'nother subject. The reality of it is I grew up in one of the best places on earth, during a unique time in history. The lessons I learned and the Game I was taught made me into a real gangsta'. So I wouldn't trade it in for all the Thizz on earth.

As a matter of fact, let me tell y'all about one of those unique lessons I learned as an adolescent. This gem manifested over a dice game that took place inside the garage at my momma's house when I was around 13 or 14 years old. I still remember that day vividly. It had been raining all morning, so the streets were wet and the sky was grey.

The garage door was wide open. Someone's boom box was on, so music was on in the background. If I recall correctly, someone was playing some Run DMC. The dice game was poppin'. All my uncles and big cousins were in there playing with other older cuddies.

The energy was turnt' up. Niggaz was talking shit, snapping they fingers and blowing on the dice before tossing 'em on the concrete. Side bets were being yelled out. Everything was fast, if you weren't up to speed you'd get left behind real quick.

I grew up playing craps. Everyone I knew played dice. Me and the louies would spend hours shaking them thangs. It didn't matter where we were at. You could be at school in the bathrooms or the hallways. Or, on the block, at the store, or someone's house, if some dice got pulled out, the cuddies would be with it.

This particular game, in my momma's garage was different, though. I always shot dice with my niggaz. We'd play for change, singles and the occasional five dollar bill. This game was with all older Cuddies and their bets were five's, ten's and twenties. Not only was the amount of money higher than what I was used to, the game was faster and more aggressive.

Even though I was a young nigga, I was still in the thick of things. I was in the circle with the sharks, squatting down watching everything.

I was soaking it all up when my uncle Peeda was like, "Let Dre shoot!" He gave me a five dollar bill and said, "It's on you, cuddy. Do ya' thang, young nigga!"

When Unc' handed me the dice I was happy as fuck! I didn't show it, though. Yeah, I was amidst family and friends, but that didn't matter. Something I learned early was playing craps was about making bread.

There's nothing funny when it comes to making money. I saw guys lose their cars, jewelry and rent money at a dice game. But, I've also seen cats win enough to drive off the lot with foreign whips with numbers on the back.

On the flip side, I've seen dice games end in fistfights. Gunshots and chalk lines happen too. Don't' get me wrong, the cuddies is savages, but I was safe. Nevertheless, in my head, every throw of the dice is serious business.

I held my breath on that first roll. It was as if the whole world slowed down when I watched the dice dance across the cement. Then, when I saw the fo' and the trey, I exhaled.

I hit!

I couldn't believe it. I took them two five's and bet back immediately. All my concentration was on the next throw.

I threw an eight. On the next roll, one of the dice landed on a two, the other gave me the six I needed. Suddenly, cuddies started giving me props. I heard 'em making comments bout my hand being hot. When I got to forty dollars, I crapped out, bringing me back to twenty. I was hot, but I made up for it when the dice made it back to me.

I blew on the dice before I threw 'em again. Then, bam! I hit an eleven. I didn't crap out again until I got to a hundred and twenty-five dollars. I wasn't even mad when I had to give 'em up that time. The stack in my hand was too fat for me to complain.

In my excitement I pulled away from the group. No one noticed me since they were all caught up in the moment. After counting the cash I ran inside where my momma was in the kitchen with my aunties and their friends.

"Momma! Look! I just won this!" I exclaimed.

She was closing the refrigerator when I ran into the kitchen. As soon as she turned around and saw all the crumpled bills in my hand, her eyes widened in surprise. Then she smiled with a certain sparkle in her eyes and told me to follow her into her bedroom.

After closing the door she said, "Boy, how much you got?"

Proudly, I said, "Over a hundred, momma!"

"Give me the hundred so I can hold it for you. You never wanna hold too much money on you, Dre. The police and jackers are always looking for someone to rob, so you never hold your money bag on you."

"Gotchu!"

Without any sort of hesitation, I counted out a C-note, gave it to her then ran back out to the garage. I jumped straight into the pool of piranhas with nothing but money on my mind. By then, the group as a whole had gotten louder. Outside, the rain was flooding the streets. More people had came, filling up the whole garage and all their attention was on the rambunctious dice game at the back of the garage.

I was really feeling myself by the time them thangs made their way back into my paws. That's when I started talking shit just like I did against the niggaz I usually played. I talked that slick shit, shook the dice and tossed 'em like a real Crestside representa'!

Seven after seven hit that pavement! If I didn't hit a seven, it was an eleven. It got to the point where my uncle Peeda was yelling shit like, "That's my mothafuckin' nephew right there! On-my-momma, y'all betta not bet against my young nigga!" To me, he said, "Get that paper, cuddy!"

When my turn came to an end I ran back inside. But, this time, instead of going in all loud, I got my momma's attention and met her in the bedroom discreetly. As soon as she shut the door, I pulled out my stack and checked what I had. There was close to three hundred dollars so I gave her two then ran back out there with the rest.

This time, when I got the dice there was a group of my relatives who wouldn't bet against me. Nigga's were taking side bets that I'd hit. Someone handed me a joint. I hit it, passed it, then threw them thangs. It got to the point where people started cheering every time I hit my number. I had never played in a game that big so the experience of that much excitement was new to a young nigga like myself. I ate it up like a real champ!

I ended up wit' a chunky pile of bills on the ground in front of me. Some of it was in my hand, some of it was under my foot, and some was around the circle for all the side bets I had going on. By the time I crapped out, I had the biggest stack of bills I ever had. What I should've done was stuck to the script. I should've brought my winnings to my momma. That's not what happened, though.

Everything was moving so fast, I didn't even think about taking my earnings to my momma. I placed bets against anybody who had the dice. On top of that, I was taking a gang of side bets. That's what really hurt my pockets. When it came back around for me to shoot, I just knew I was gonna blow back up! I took the dice in the palm of my hand, shook 'em, blew on 'em, and threw 'em...

Snake eyes! I hit two ones which meant I lost my bread, but I still kept the dice.

"Dayum, Dre!" a couple people behind me said.

I know they all saw how short my stack was getting. I don't think anyone was really paying attention to the fact that I had been tucking my cheese with my ol' girl. I put the rest of my stash on the next roll… and lost.

Unc' patted me on the shoulder and said, "You did good, lil nigga."

"I know, Unc'. I ain't done, though. I'll be back."

I remember him giving me an inquisitive look before I took off. He must've thought I was broke, too. But I wasn't. I went inside and signaled for my momma to meet me in her room again.

As soon as we had a little privacy I said, "Momma, gimme some money."

"What? Why"

"I lost what I had. I need some of my money so I can get back in the game."

The moment I finished that statement I immediately saw something in my moms' demeanor change. Now, before I go on with this story, I gotta tell y'all something about my ol' girl. She's one of them strong Black mothers who didn't have a problem slapping the taste out my mouth. For the most part, she was loving and supportive. But when I got on her nerves she had a quick left hook and it stung. I'm not saying that was her go-to. But I did know the signs that let me know when I was treading on thin ice.

The way her eyes squinted when she said, "No" told me she was gonna stand her ground.

"No?"

"You heard me! Now, get out my way. I got some pork chops on the stove."

I was blocking the door. I didn't move. This was my money, so I couldn't understand what all that was about. "Momma, that's my money. I need it, man!"

"No!" she said more forcefully. "Yeah, I know you gave me that money. I also know what you want it for. I'm just not gonna give it to you! Now, get out my mothafuckin' face before I slap you into next week! You's a degenerate-ass gambler just like ya' good-for-nothing father! Get out my way, boy!"

Needless to say, I was hot! Hotter than an Alabama summer! Moms' pushed me out the way, and left me standing there looking stupid. I made a killin' at that dice game, and she just took my money. It felt like she jacked me for my hard earned cash. That was moms', though. I couldn't do shit about it.

I had to get up outta there before I said something stupid. Instead of walking through the garage, I left the house through the front door, making sure I slammed that mothafucka' on the my way out. I wasn't trying to get clowned in front of the whole neighborhood, so I got up out there before shit escalated.

The game is like that sometimes. You can fly to heights you've never reached before without knowing how you got there. The Catch 22 is that you can lose everything if you fly too close to the sun...

CHAPTER

TWO

"When the streets mold ya', you grow up to be a soldia'!"
-Mac Dre

I was hot when my ol' girl did that. I worked hard for that cheese. And, she just took it for no reason!
You know how quick you gotta be when you playing craps against that many niggaz? The fact that I was the youngest shooter in the circle had already put me at a disadvantage.

At the time, I was tall for may age so it wasn't like the cuddies were towering over me. Still, though, a fast dice game can get aggressive. Some guys will try to pick up the dice before everybody else can see if they crapped out. Others will reach they nasty-ass mitts across the circle, tryna snatch the cash up, claiming they hit their number. All kinds of cons get implemented. So you gotta be quick on your toes.

So, yeah... I took off walking. I was in my usual attire of T-shirt and Levis. My Addidas were spotless and the high-top fade was crispy.

At the time, we lived in a two bedroom house on Cynthia Ave. The Crest was a residential neighborhood built for working class white folks in the 1950's. You can tell by the name that was given to the subdivision: Country Club Crest.

By the time moms' and I moved to the Crest it was a ghetto. There weren't that many white families living in North Vallejo at the time. We got the house because my ol' girl got her Section 8 voucher. Most of my friends had Section 8, too. I always figured that's how we inherited the Crest.

The hood was always off the chain. To me and the Cuddies, it was like a playground where everyday brought a new adventure. The main concept of life in the Crest was getting money. The options, or lines of stacking chips were damn near limitless because the neighborhood was really poppin'. If you were into flockin', you could hit houses. If you sold Cream you could bleed the block.

Most of the louies were Mac's. We'd get it off a bitch's back. Straight up! You meet a breezy that's square and become her Prince Charming. Get up in her ear and tell her what she wants to hear. Once her defenses are lowered, you spread them legs like the letter 'V' so you can overdose her with that letter 'D." After that, you got yourself you very own ATM machine.

In my 'hood, all the Avenues run from East to West. The streets twist and turn like most do in the Bay. Nevertheless, the one consistency is all the streets run North to South. Most of them have names after people like Christopher Way, Amelia Street, or Wendy Street. All the twist and turns can confuse an outsider, but a real Crestsider knows the 'hood like the back of his hand.

It didn't take long for me to run into the cuddies. There was a spot on Amelia Street a few blocks away from my house where we always bled the block together. Curt, Jamal and Coolio were three of my closest friends.

We called ourselves the Romper Room, based on a TV show most of y'all probably never heard of. We weren't the only members of this Double R clique. There were like 15 to 20 of us. But we all had our specific circles within the larger cipher.

Jamal was one of the first cuddies I met when I moved to the Crest. J-Diggs, as most people know him, was dark skinned and tall like me. His momma was friends with my momma so we always stayed at one another's house when we were kids. When school started, we just naturally stuck together pushing like we were brothers.

Curt, or Kilo Curt, was another one of the louies who was there before all the sex, money and murder. He was a year older than me and J. We were all the same height and stature though. I remember the first time I met Curt was at Borges Park. I had went up there on Christmas morning with a brand new remote control car that my momma had bought me. There were a few other young niggaz my age up there. They were at the basketball courts and I didn't really know them. They all had they own remote controlled cars too so I went up there to fuck around with them. One thing got to another and they tried jacking me for mine. Two of them started packing me out while the third one ran off with my remote controlled car.

Kilo had been watching the whole thing play out and came up with a plan. While the guys who were jumping me had their attention taken, he snatched up their cars and tossed 'em in some bushes. After that, brody came to my aide. With his assistance, we whooped them dudes. In their haste to get up outta there, they didn't even think to look for their cars. When it was all said and done, we both had our own cars and a new found friendship.

I met Coolio in 3rd grade. Coolio is shorter than the rest of us. Plus, he's light skinned. That's why we call 'im Unda Dogg. He's always in the midst of everything from sports to bitches and fistfights. And he never let nothing stop him from stuntin' on a sucka. He always had a chip on his shoulder. It didn't matter how big a mothafucka' is, if they shot any shade in his way whatsoever, he was catching that fade. That's my nigga for life! On 3 C's!

Like I said earlier, there's other cuddies in the Romper Room. Mac Mall was one of 'em. But I'll tell you 'bout brody a little later.

When I hit the block and saw the louies, I immediately felt better. It was always all love. We gave each other dap and J passed me a Camel wit' no filter. He must've seen it in my face because the first thing he said was, "What's wrong witchu', cuddy?"

That's when Coolio chimed in, "Yeah, nigga! What's up? We gotta get on somebody, or what?"

"Naw, man," I replied after puffing on the cigarette. "I'm just hot 'cause moms' just chipped me for some bread I hit for in the dice game at my house."

"Y'all shootin' over there?" Coolio. "Let's go!"

"Naw, cuddy. It's all my uncles and them. They let me get in, and I hit 'em something nice. I kept stacking my chips with my momma, then when I got hit she wouldn't give me my money back. I don't wanna go back over there right now. That shit got me hot!"

"Dayum, cuddy," Jay and Coolio both said.

Then Curt slid into the convo', "How much was it?"

"Five hundred," I lied.

"Fuuuck!" they said.

"That's ya' ol' girl, tho', cuddy." continued Curt. I could always count on him to calm me down. He was a thinker. The cuddy was always strategic and analytic in everything he did. "Did she leave you with anything?"

"Naw."

For a minute, we all got quiet. See, like I said before, most of the homies had someone in their immediate family who was on that hard white rock. At one point or another, everyone of us had something stolen or taken from us by a close family member. It was just a part of our lives so they could all relate to how I was feeling right then and there.

"Here," Jay said. He handed me a rock wrapped in plastic.

"Huh," Coolio said. He did the same.

Curt gave me one too.

"Good lookin', cuddies ." I popped 'em in my mouth and held them in my cheek.

I didn't come looking for a handout. I knew if I needed one, the louies would come through for a nigga. All the cuddies sold Cream. We was young at the time. None of us were getting rich, but selling dope did give us enough to buy a new pair of shoes or a fresh haircut when we needed it. For some of us, selling a bag of weed, or a rock, made the difference between going to sleep hungry or full.

"So, what's up wit' y'all?" I asked. "Any money out here?"

"Naw," Jay replied. "It's slow as fuck out here. Ain't no money been coming through. But, this nigga, Curt been talking 'bout going by Nini's house. Tia's over there, too."

Nini and Tia were two of the prettiest girls in the neighborhood. They were best friends who always had the flyest gear and newest hairstyles. They were popular, but they were also older than us and never gave any of us any play.

"Curt?!" I said. "Nigga, them bitches liable to slam the door as soon as they see your Gremlin'-lookin' ass!"

"I know you ain't talkin'," Coolio started. "Can't nobody get a word in when your big-ass inner tube lips get to flappin'!"

Everybody started laughing and I couldn't blame them. I do got some big-ass lips. But I had to clap back anyway,

"Unda Dogg, Mac'n consist of a fly nigga spittin' smooth shit in a bitch ear. You ain't even finna speak up if we did go over there."

That's when Curt got back in the mix, "Fuck you, cuddy. Me an Coolio can go over there right now and fuck both them bitches!"

I looked at Jay, giving him a look that asked, "Can you believe these fools?" and he said, "It don't count if they sleepin' and you're standing outside they window with a jar of Vaseline and ya' pants around ya' ankles, cuddy!"

We all busted out laughing at that one. Curt got a little hot, but he didn't say anything. You had to have thick skin when you pushed with the louies because we stayed wit' the fuck around. As far as talking slick shit went, it was no holds barred in the Romper Room.

After that, we started walking towards the local corner store, King's Market. It really isn't a grocery store as much as it's a liquor store. But that's what it's called. You can catch the cuddies there killing time. It was a cool spot to get a few dollars if you had some weed or cream. It was also a spot for sideshows on the weekends. On any given Friday or Saturday night, you can catch the Romper Room posted up outside popping that gold label game at bitches.

On that afternoon there weren't too many people out and about. The streets were still wet even though the drizzle dried up. Then, when we were about a block away, I heard some beat knocking in the distance. The other cuddies must've heard it too because we all stopped and kinda scanned the block.

It was two cars coming up the street from behind us. The first one was a compact, two-door Ford Escort. The driver and passenger looked like some bummy white dudes. I immediately recognized 'em. They were smokers who regularly came to the 'hood to cop.

A few car lengths behind the Escort was one of the freshest Cadillacs in the Crest. It was root beer brown, sitting on Trues and Vogues. We already knew exactly who owned it. It was an older Pimp homey by the name of Lay-Low. The cuddy, Mike-Mike (who was later known as The Mac) was in the passenger seat. Mike-Mike was our age. When they saw us, they slowed down and pulled up to the curb.

Jay saw me eyeing the knocks in the Escort and said, "Go ahead, cuddy. You the one who just took the loss."

I replied, "A'ight."

I then made eye contact with the driver of the compact Ford and signaled for him to pull over. After that, I scanned the block. Once I was sure the coast was clear, I ran up to the passenger window and made a $20 sale.

By the time I turned back around, the cuddies were all posted up around the 'Lac. The owner of the Bro-ham was a big homey from the hood. Everything about him was upper echelon. The cuddies my age had a lot of love for him because anytime he saw us in traffic, he'd stop and lace us with some real game.

Lay-Low was Mike-Mike's dad's friend. Mike's pops' had been locked up his whole life, so Lay-Low had kinda adopted him in a way. Mike-Mike was around Coolio's age, but he was tall like the rest of us. This mattered because he looked older than he really was. At an early age he was exposed to pimpin'. He was laced so tight at such an early point in his life that he was ahead of the rest of us in many ways.

It was as if he was being cultivated to become the sharpest Mac the 'hood had ever seen. What made it so cold was he was one of the louies! He spent a lot more time with OG's but he was our age so he'd always bring back the game he learned. There were countless evenings in the 'hood when we'd all be crowded around Mike-Mike listening to his latest out-of-town pimpin' escapades.

Later on, when I named myself Mac Dre, it was from a loving admiration for the cuddy, Mike-Mike. He was the first rapper out the Crest who actually dropped an album. He's the one who gave us the game on how to penetrate the music industry.

The Bay has had all kinds of rappers doing their thang. From Too Short, RBL Posse to Live Wire and my very own, Thizz Ent. The music always brought us money, but most of us were hustlers. As the game got deeper, the music industry became a cloaking device that camouflaged our illicit movements.

What I can say, coming from someone who really lived it, is the Mac, Michael Robinson was who showed the Crest how it was really supposed to be done.

He took his street money and had albums pressed. He paid to have posters made, Radio DJ's were paid off to play his music, too. The cuddy travelled all over the Bay pushing his music. He set the stage for all the cuddies who came after him. It's fucked up how his life ended, but I'll tell y'all 'bout all that a little later.

As soon as I walked up, Mike-Mike greeted me with a gangsta's embrace. Lay-Low was already holding court with the cuddies.

"What's up, player?" I asked Mike.

"Doin' my thang, cuddy. Try'na stack this bread. You know, it's all on a bitch. I got me a little Filipino thang from Frisco whose been droppin' it in my lap."

"Naw! For real, cuddy!?" I asked excitedly. "You got a hoe-bitch?"

"Yeah, Dre. Check her out. She's in the back seat."

Bruh led me to the rear of the 'Lac and tilted his head toward her. She was a bad, sexy thang, too. She looked like she was in her early twenties.

"She ain't gunna look at you, 'cause I got her trained, cuddy."

I shook my head in amazement. It seemed like every time I saw bruh he was on some upper echelon shit.

"Cuddy," he said. "I'm 'bout to get in the rap game. I just a met a producer from Frisco named Kyree. We 'bout to get some studio time so I can lay down some tracks."

"Put that on something!"

"On my momma, cuddy! I'ma put this Mac'n on vinyl and see where it takes me. You need to start writing, Dre. Every time we be freestylin', you kill the cipher."

"I don't know... You think so?"

"On my momma, Dre."

"I guess I might try some shit."

"Check it out, cuddy. I'ma tell you like the older louies been tellin' me: Rappin' aint nothing but Mac'n. The only difference is you spittin' ya' propaganda so the world can hear. This life we was born into is gangsta, Dre. It's giving us an "ism" the rest of the world can't compete with. All I'm doin' is writing it all down. Then I deliver it like a real Crestside representa'. You can do it too!"

I nodded my head. "Bet dat! I'ma start writing some shit down."

After that, we went towards the front of the car where Lay-Low was seated on the 'hood lacing the louies with that A-1 game.

"I see y'all bleeding the block. As you should, but let me pull ya' coattail to a little somethin'-somethin', young cuddies. When you out here committin' felonies, you don't wanna carry 'em on you. Use your head. Regardless of whether the rocks are in ya' mouth, ya ass cheeks, or shoes; if the rollers find 'em on you, you're goin' to jail. What y'all need to do is recruit you some young bitches to hold ya' sac. Ya' hear me? When was the last time any of you seen the Jakes searching a bitch your age?"

No one replied.

"Ya' see what I'm sayin'! Get y'all some PYT's and have 'em bleed the block for you. Now, that's enough game for today. Me and the young P gotta bend a few more corners."

After that, Lay-Low and Mike-Mike got back in the 'Lac and slid up the block.

That's how it was in the 'hood. The Crest didn't breed no haters. It was like we were all apart of an extended family of pimps, players and hustlers...

CHAPTER

THREE

"Do it moving, 'cause slow niggaz get left."
-Mac Dre

We made it to King's Market, bought a few vittles then started walking back through the 'hood. Since we weren't really headed anywhere in particular so we took a detour down a street we didn't usually take.

I can still remember that afternoon like it was yesterday. The streets were drying up from all the rain that fell earlier in the day. It was cool, but it was about to turn up real quick.

You gonna hear me refer to my 'hood as a ghetto. That's because it was, in the sense that a bunch of poor minorities live in one area of the city. Yet, the Crest wasn't a slum with housing projects.

A lot of the cuddies lived in houses because our momma's had Section 8. The homes in our section of the city were originally built for middle class families, but at some point the white folks migrated. When they left, Black families from all over the Bay Area started moving in. It's the same thing that happened to Sacramento in the early 2000's, but we'll get to that in due time.

The reason I brought all this up is to give you a picture of the terrain. The 'hood still has a lot of middle class working people living in it. That's why so many of us come up off flocking. If you don't know what that is, it's burglary. Most of the young cuddies our age were into flocking at that time. Whenever we skipped school, or just so happened to be presented with an opportunity, we capitalized on it.

The crew I ran with was really wit' the shit back then. We called ourselves the Romper Room. Not everyone from the Crest were Romper Room affiliates, though. Our clique consisted of about 15 of us. We were all between the ages of 14 and 21 when we went stupid-doo-doo-dumb. As we got older, we became a force to be reckoned with because we had no problem with stompin' off brand niggaz out.

Something I've learned about the Game is there's levels to this shit. It gets deeper as you mature and become more sophisticated in the streets. The transition some make into the upper echelon of the underworld doesn't just depend on your age and maturity. It can also be affected by the company you keep.

As far as the Romper Room was concerned we were all around the same age. That changed as the calendars slipped by. Later on, as we got older, we had young cuddies like Mac Mall, who was 15 years old, doing the same shit as the cuddies who were six and seven years older than him.

During that time in our push, my circle within a circle specialized in bleeding the block and flockin'. So, when we passed a house with telltale signs telling us it was empty, our flocking antennas went up immediately.

Coolio was the first to recognize the opportunity. We were all leisurely strolling up the block when the cuddy stopped in his tracks in front of a big, blue, two-story house. It had a two car garage with a stack of old newspapers in the driveway.

"Hey!" Coolio said. "Y'all see that?"

Jay must've saw the papers at the same time as the Unda Dogg because he stopped and said, "Check it out! That's at least four papers!"

"You know what dat means," I said.

We all stopped walking by then. I started scanning the block for any neighbors who might have been outside. Everything looked cool, too. The coast was clear, no one was in sight. This wasn't our first B & E so we knew the proper procedure.

"We clear?" Curt asked.

Everyone said, "Yes," so it was on. Me, Curt, and Jay walked up the driveway and posted up in front of the garage. The point was to be out of sight when Coolio went up to the door.

Since Da Unda dogg was shorter than the rest of us, we utilized his baby-faced features. He went up to the door and ran the bell. He had a paper in his hand, so if anyone answered, he'd tell them he noticed the extra newspapers in the driveway and wanted to know if he could have one for himself.

While he was at the door, the rest of us scanned the block for possible witnesses. It was starting to become evening. The sky was orange and getting darker by the minute. I knew no one came to the door because I heard Coolio knocking on it. I remember feeling my adrenaline starting to pump. It was about to go down.

After a few moments, I peeked around the corner of the garage. Coolio saw me and gave the sign that everything was clear.

"C'mon, y'all," I told the others. The next phase of the juxt was on Jay. Jay was the stockiest one out of us, so he was always the one who kicked in the doors.

"BOOM! BOOM! KRSSHHH!"

The door splintered open and we blitzed it.

"I got upstairs!" I announced on my way in.

"Me too!" Coolio said.

Curt and Jay took the bottom half of the house. It really didn't matter who ended up where because in the end we'd split the loot evenly. Most of the time, if you flocked a house with some off brand niggaz, you couldn't trust 'em to have honor amongst thieves. But, these was my niggaz. We kept it a hunnid wit' each other at all times.

The purpose of calling out a section was to cover the most space in the shortest amount of time. Since most of the houses in the Crest were built with the same layout, the blueprint was already embedded in our heads. I already knew to take a right at the top of the stairs because it's where the master bedroom would be. To the left: there'd be two smaller bedrooms. I took the bigger room while Curt covered the others.

I had a cold method to my madness. When ever I hit a bedroom, the first spot I searched was the dresser. After checking all the drawers, I'd look under the bed. The closest was always last.

The first and most important rule to flocking is *Never get caught*. Every move you make has to coincide with an exit strategy. This means you gotta be quick. Everyone has to be in and out the house within three to five minutes.

The second rule was *Only take what you can carry in your hands.* This means you can't take big items like TV's, furniture, or large appliances. If you can't carry it by yourself, it doesn't leave the house.

Whenever the cuddies hit a house we look for cash, jewelry and guns. If the house had a safe we'd take that too. You'd be surprised how many homes had all those things laying around.

I'm like a bloodhound in those types of situations. It doesn't take me long to find shiny things. In less than two minutes, I found a shoebox on the top shelf in the closet. The moment I saw it, the cat burglar in me knew I found a prize. Then, just as I reached up and grabbed it, Coolio rushed in the room clutching on a gold watch in one hand and a necklace in the other.

"You got anything?" he asked.

"I think so."

I opened the box and a Kool Aid smile eclipsed my face. The cuddy must've sensed the vibe 'cause he came closer to get a better look.

"Yeah, cuddy," I said." I got a strap! C'mon, let's go!"

It was chrome revolver and it went straight into my waistband. After that, we went downstairs. The pistol was a prize. I was hella happy. I could sell it or keep it. Either option was a win.

When we reached the bottom of the stairs I found Jay at the door leading to the garage. His hands were empty, but he had a smirk on his face.

"Where's Curt?" I asked, wondering if their luck had been as good as ours.

"He found some keys on the wall in the kitchen," he replied. "We might have a stolo to mob in if they work."

That's when Curt rushed back in from the garage. He was wide-eyed, like it was Christmas morning, or something.

"I got a Caprice, y'all! Check it out!" he exclaimed.

We all went into the garage, turned on the light and saw a brand new, all blue Chevy Caprice. It was spotless. The paint was wet. The guts were pristine; clean like granny's living room!

Stealing cars was another pastime for the cuddies. There were times when the whole Romper Room would mob through the city in a caravan of stolos. None of us had plugs to a chop shop back then, though. So since stolen cars didn't really generate funds they weren't much of a priority. Nevertheless, there we were, with a brand new Chevy and the keys to start it. It was mandatory we took that bitch!

Even though I already knew the answer, I still popped the question: "What y'all wanna do?"

"What're we waiting for?" Jay said. "That bitch got a big-ass trunk. Start loading the TV's and VCR's in it!"

We all stood there for a second. It went against one of the rules of flocking to take TV's, yet it became an option the moment we got the car. That's why we all hesitated for a second. But, after a while, it seemed to have sunk into our minds all at the same time because we suddenly jumped to action all at the same time.

We rushed back inside and ran in different directions. The TV in the living room was heavy but I grabbed it. Unda Dogg took the VCR and somehow put it on top of a microwave before making his way back into the garage. Jay and Curt took the house stereo and Nintendo console with all the video games.

The trunk was loaded with loot in record time. At first, we couldn't shut it but the cuddies moved some shit around. In the end, we made it work.

Since it was Curt who found the keys, he ended up being the designated driver. As we got older, Curt became our getaway driver whenever we needed one. The cuddy got handles, but he wasn't as skilled back then as he ended up being later on in years. I took the front passenger seat next to him. And the cuddies hopped in the back.

"Coolio, open the garage, cuddy!" Curt said after starting the engine. Obviously, no one had thought of that.

The Unda Dogg hopped out, ran behind the car and started struggling with the garage door. Something was wrong. It was taking too long for him to lift it.

Jay mumbled something under his breath that sounded like, "What-da-fuck is going on?"

Then Coolio hollared out: "This mothafucka' stuck!"

"Damn!" we all said in unison.

A decision had to be made quick. We had already been in that house way too long. On top of that, my brain was already working overtime on figuring out how much money we were gonna make off all the loot we were taking.

Not to mention all the Nintendo games. We were definitely keeping all of those. I knew everyone else must've been contemplating the same thing because no one budged.

The silence was thick but Kilo Curt cut straight to it. "Get in, cuddy!"

"It's locked from the outside, bruh!" Coolio replied.

"Fuck all'at! Get back in the car!" Curt said. As soon as Coolio got back in the whip, Curt looked at us and said, "We 'bout to get on some A-Team shit, cuddies. Y'all ready?"

The look in the louie's eyes told me all I needed to know. I held on to my seat and said, "Fuck it! Let's ride!"

Curt put the Chevy in drive, then inched as close to the back of the garage as he could. The front bumper was literally touching the wall. Then he slapped that bitch into reverse and stomped his foot on the gas.

The rear wheel drive spun them tires, causing them to screech like some hyenas before they gripped the concrete. Once they got their footing, the Caprice took flight! Slamming into the garage door with enough force to shatter the lock, bustin' that bitch wide open!

The snapping of wood and crashing of the garage door when it slammed up against the top of the garage was loud. Yet the squealing of the tires as we hit the driveway and slid into the street was even louder. The Cuddy slid us onto the pavement sideways before slapping the gear shift in drive and smoking up the block.

"Yee!" we yelled in triumph!

We hit the block on a whole 'nother trip. I turned up the radio, changed it from the country station it was on, to 106.1 KMEL. The DJ had a hip-hop mix on with Digital Underground leading the way. The louies got lit. We all started hopping around, dancing to the music.

I don't know if it was the sound of the screeching tires, or the smell of burning rubber; but no one said anything about stashing the shit we took from the house. Instead of unloading the loot and ditching the Chevy, we did donuts and hit a few blocks sideways.

After a while, we drove past King's Market, saw Jamal's uncle posted up with a few more Cuddies and decided to double back and post up. As soon as we pulled up, all eyes were on us. I'm telling y'all; the ride was clean!

King's Market was a real Country Club Crest spot. You didn't need ID to get a 40oz of Old E. We parked the Chevy like we owned it. Then we pulled out, got some intoxicants and loitered with the louies.

The night was young and dark just like the cuddies. I remember a dice game was about to kick off on the side of the market 'til somebody said: "That bitch ain't hot!"

Of course, *that bitch* was the Caprice and the statement was taken as a full on challenge by Kilo Curt. Even though the car wasn't his, and he had only been driving it less than an hour he felt the need to defend its honor.

"I bet I'll smoke up the whole block!" he announced.

"You got handles like that, little Cuddy?" Jay's uncle Jermaine asked.

"Do Cheetahs got spots?" Curt replied.

And that was an official call to arms. Coolio, Jay and I hopped in the ride with Curt and proceeded to officially stunt. With the music turnt' up as loud as the stock radio allowed it, Curt pulled out the parking spot and started wildin' out!

While still in the Market's parking lot, he did a standstill that engulfed the lot with thick white smoke!

"This bitch got posi! Both tires is smokin', cuddy!" Coolio yelled.

"Yee! Yee! Yee!" the louies on the block yelled.

The Caprice did a slow crawl towards the entrance of the parking lot. The smoke from the brand new tires was thick and light bright. Then Curt let off the gas for a second, spun the steering wheel and punched it into the street. He hit the four-way sideways and went straight into the series of figure-eight donuts.

Over and over again, we spun in loud, pavement staining circles. The streets were still moist from the showers earlier in the day. So that helped with the level of spinning we were doing. But one thing that couldn't be denied was the power from the V8 under the hood of that car. That bitch was hot!

After disrupting the night with screeching tires and thick smoke, the Chevy took off in a sprint. From there we hit every spot in the Crest. Everywhere cuddies congregated we spun tires and hit donuts.

We went stupid-doo-doo-dumb that night. We were so young and wild that no one had the sense to slow things down. We all knew we were joy ridin' in a stolo; that the stolen car came from a house in the 'hood; and that we were making a hella-hella, big-ass scene. None of us cared though. We were young Crestsiders in our own world.

Then somebody said, "Damn!"

Less than a second later, a patrol car's lights lit up the interior of the ride. A familiar chirp from the cop car sounded. Then a siren woke up the rest of the night.

"It's McGraw!" Jamal yelled.

McGraw was the neighborhood overseer. He was and continues to be to this day, a real bitch! He's the type of cop that lives for whoopin' niggaz asses then hittin' 'em wit' a charge for dope he planted on 'em. He was a certified bitch!

Everyone from the North Pole knew that honky. Story had it that he grew up in the Crest and went to school with the older Cuddies. They used to bully his ass hella bad and one of the neighborhood Mac's turnt' out his little sister.

This mothafuckin' punk-bitch had a full on vendetta for all fly niggaz. As the years went on, he ended up targeting the Romper Room in the worst way. But, let's not move ahead of ourselves.

We were suddenly caught between a rock and a hard place. There were two options: stop or run. We all looked at Curt since he was behind the wheel. The next move was on him.

As he stared out the back window through the rearview mirror, he said, "I'm not going to the hall's tonight, y'all!"

CHAPTER FOUR

"Dumb outlaw on a crooked path."
-Mac Dre

I felt the front of the car raise up when the cuddy stomped on the gas peddle. Curt leaned in towards the steering wheel and started driving like Jeff Gordon. It instantly felt like we were in a movie. But this time, the crooks were 'bout to get away.

"Fuck dat honky!" Jay yelled.

"Don't even trip, Cuddy!" Curt said. "Just get ready to hop out and hit some fences when I tell y'all."

We were moving fast through a residential area. Curt took a hard left, causing the tires to screech as the Chevy slid in the direction he wanted it to. The cop was on us, though. He was close enough for everyone to see his face. In retrospect, we should've realized since we could see him then he could obviously see us too. At the time, though, none of that mattered. Curt was flying down Round Street.

"Get ready, y'all!" he yelled. "I'ma let y'all know when it's good to get your hundred yard dash on!"

The radio was loud, playing an LL Cool J song called *Who's Bad!* On top of that, the siren behind us was extra loud, waking up the whole turf.

Curt almost sideswiped a parked car when he snatched a hard left on Wendy Street! It slid us all to the right side of the Chevy. All the weight in the trunk made us fishtail, too. But Curt had handles. He stayed in control as he raced through the night.

"Y'all ready?" he asked again.

Jay said, "We gotta split up. McGraw's by himself, so he ain't gonna be able to run in four directions at once."

Then, just as the words left the cuddy's mouth another cop car joined the chase. The new pig hit the block in front of us; heading in our direction. I saw the scowl on his face as we raced past him. He had to slam on his brakes so he could make a U-turn behind McGraw in order for him to join the chase.

"I'm bout to hit Mark Street!" announced the cuddy. "As soon as I bend this corner, everybody hop out!"

My shoes were laced, ready for this foot race. Then, about twenty yards from the stop sign, McGraw bumped the rear of the Caprice with the nose of his car. He spun us! The Chevy started hitting 360's like the T-Cup ride at the State Fair!

Still, the louies were on point! Curt yelled, "Y'all ready!?" and one of us replied with the turf call, "Yee!"

"KRSSHHH!"

The Chevy crashed into a parked car before sliding into the curb. The Chevy hadn't even fully stopped before my feet hit the pavement. McGraw's headlights hit me as I ran across the closest lawn on my way towards a fence.

Everybody split up. I didn't have no time to see where they went. All I knew was I was hoping fence after fence as fast as possible. I was on a roll! It looked like I made a clean escape until I hit the third yard and found myself face to face with an big-ass German Shepard!

He must've heard me coming because he was right there when I hopped off the top of the gate surrounding his yard. He was in full attack mode, too. Hair standing up; teeth bearing'; low growl coming from his chest.

"Oh shit!" I whispered. That mothafucka' was inching towards me. "Calm down, little buddy. I don't want no problems."

I was trying to talk Cujo down until I heard some noise coming from the yard I just came from. It had to be McGraw, I thought to myself. The footsteps were too heavy for it not to be. The moment I heard him hit the fence, I took off again.

Cujo didn't waste no time, either. That mothafucka' cut towards me just as quick as I took off. I know my adrenalin was pumping extra thick 'cause I was on my Flash Gordon tip.

Cujo was on me! As soon as I was within hopping distance of the fence, I jumped up and grabbed the top of it. He sprung into the air right behind me, locking onto my shoe! The pressure of his bite almost took my left shoe off, but I kicked 'im in the nose. That moved actually saved me. It bought me enough freedom to make it over the fence.

"Stop! Stop, you little nigger!" McGraw yelled in pursuit of ya' boy. Then I heard a growl and a sudden scuffle. McGraw screamed, "AHHHH!"

My foot game never wavered. I was gone! Hoping Cujo would buy me enough time to get away. Then I heard the shots:

POP! POP! POP!

Later on, I found out McGraw killed the dog. But I swear, that night, I thought he was busting at me!

My whole life, moms' had been telling me not to run from the police. For as long as I could remember, I was told the police had a free pass to kill Blacks who ran from them. So, even though I knew Cujo was in the mix, when I heard them shots in the background I automatically assumed the racist cracka' was bustin' at me.

When I made it home I went straight to my room and laid down on my bed. That night, as I stared up at the ceiling I kept replaying the sound of the gunshots in my head.

At some point, I remembered the pistol in my back pocket. Somehow,

it didn't fall out while I was hitting fences. I took it out and studied it. It was beautiful. A shiny chrome piece with a wooden handle. There were six hollow heads in the chamber. Holding it in my hand made me think of the way I felt when McGraw squeezed his trigger. That's when I understood the power of a pistol.

I gave my body enough time to calm down from the adrenaline rush I had just experienced before I tucked the revolver under the mattress. My throat was hella-hella dry so I went to the kitchen to get something to drink.

Making sure I didn't make too much noise, I slowly crept through the hallway. But when I passed by my momma's room I knew she was up. Her light was on, it was shining from underneath her door. She had some Isley Brothers playing in the background, too. She obviously had someone in there with her which was probably why she hadn't heard all the sirens screaming through the turf a little while earlier.

Moms' never really had a boyfriend. But she did have "friends." They usually showed up at the house on Thursdays or Fridays. Those were the days most people got their paychecks.

One thing I can say about my momma was she never really messed with people who didn't have something going for themselves. Most of the time, she'd go grocery shopping, or out to run errands after one of her friends spent the night. I wouldn't call my momma a prostitute. She really wasn't. Yet, She taught me early on that pussy had power. The power of quid pro quoi.

Her having company had most likely saved me from getting' questioned about all the drama in the streets. Technically, it wasn't that late at night. She would usually be up and moving around the house around that time of night.

If she would've seen the condition my shoes were in, that alone would've gotten me yelled at for at least an hour. It wouldn't have mattered if I bought them myself, or not. It would have been on with her.

When I made it back to my room I fell asleep pretty quick. My last thoughts were on all the money we lost in the trunk of that Chevy. The only thing I took from the heist was that pistol I had.

Maybe I'll sell it... was the last thought that escaped my mental as I fell asleep.

$$$$$

I woke up the next morning hungry as hell! My stomach was touching my back.

I got up, took a piss then went straight to the fridge. I was barefoot, in boxers with no shirt on. Half asleep, I opened the 'frigerator and found myself staring into an empty box. There was a milk container but it was empty. All the shelves were bare except for three eggs in the slots on the door.

Okay, that's a start, I thought to myself. Then I took 'em out and looked around the kitchen. No bread, but the rice cooker was on the counter. I looked inside of it. *Whala!* Some left over rice. Eggs, over easy, across some rice was a quick meal.

The frying pan was on the stove with a chunk of butter beginning to melt when I heard my momma's bedroom door open and shut. I expected to see moms' come from the hallway but it ended up being Dave. One of her "friends."

"What's up with you, Dre?"

"Nothing much," I replied. "Just fixin' something to eat. You want some?" I asked, hoping he wouldn't take me up on my offer.

"Naw. I'm good. I got some things I gotta get done this morning."

"A'ight, then, Dave."

"See ya' later."

It hit me as he left that it must've been the end of the month. I never really paid much attention to dates back then. But, I knew Dave only came around at the end of the month. At the time, I didn't know why but it always seemed to happen like that.

Dave had been coming around for years. He didn't talk much. He was cool, though. He once bought me a bike for my birthday.

The first time I met him was when my momma took me with her to his apartment. It had to have been when I was around eight or nine. As soon as we got there, he asked me if I liked lions I said, "Yeah," and he led me to the big screen television. A minute later, he had a National Geographic video playing. Next thing I knew, there was a box of Pop Tarts in my hand and a cup of milk on the coffee table in front of me. Him and my moms then disappeared into a back room until the video was over.

His presence was good for me for a couple of reasons. First, I knew my momma would be in a good mood when she woke up. Secondly, she'd most likely have enough money to go grocery shopping. The fact that she hadn't come out the room yelling and screaming told me she was oblivious to the previous night's shenanigans. That was a plus, too.

She ended up stepping into the kitchen just as I settled in at the table with my breakfast. I didn't look up, or say anything when I saw her. I was still feeling some type of way about the way she did me the day before.

She must've sensed my passive aggressiveness towards her because she said, "What's wrong wit'chu?!"

Her tone was laced with venom. Letting me know I was traversing on thin ice.

"Ain't no food in the fridge.

"You think I don't know that? I'ma fill it up today."

"With what? The money you took from me?"

I knew I shouldn't have said that the moment it left my mouth.

"What'chu say, boy!"

"Nothin', momma."

"Nawww! You said something smart, Dre. If you got something to say, get it off that bird chest of yours!"

I didn't look up.

She sat down in the seat next to mines. I wasn't blind to the fact that she was now close enough to pop me in my mouth if I tried her. So I stayed conscious of her movements.

"Dre, I've been on this earth a lot longer than you. Meaning, I can see things before you do because I've got experience. Lord knows I wish your daddy was around to teach you these things, but since he's not, it's all on me."

I still didn't say anything. The fact that she hadn't slapped or punched me yet was a good thing. But I still wasn't in the clear.

"You're reaching the age where the streets are calling you, Dre. You ain't no saint, either. I know you and friends be getting into shit. And I know I'm not gonna be able to stop you from doing certain things. But, I'm doing my best. So when I get a chance to teach you an important lesson, I'm gonna do the best I can. You listening to me, boy?!"

"Yes, momma."

"I need you to understand that I love you. I'll never do anything that isn't in your best interest. Yes, You got your uncles and your friends. But, it's really just you and me against the world! This money," she took out the roll of bread I gave her the day before. After tossing it on the table in front of me, she continued, "That shit comes and goes. But my love for you is forever! It's bulletproof! Don't ever let money come in between us again! Especially, when it's over something like money you made gambling."

"Craps ain't gambling, momma. It's hustling."

"What? Boy, what you think playing dice is what?"

"It's a hustle."

She shook her head, and started laughing. "Boy, playing craps is gambling. And gambling is an addiction. I've seen people lose everything they ever worked for in dice games they couldn't pull away from. Anyways, I didn't give this back to you yesterday because I knew the dice had cooled down. I didn't want you to lose it to the same niggaz you won it from. Now, we might never know if I was right, or not. But what we do know is you still got your money."

I reached for the billfold, but she beat me to the punch. She quickly snatched it back. Before I could say anything she took the rubber band off it and peeled off five ten dollar bills.

"I'm taking fifty for groceries. There's two-fifty left. Here you go." She reached out to hand it back to me then suddenly pulled it back. "Dre, if you're gonna be getting money in these streets, you need to learn how to save. You need to set goals for yourself. Stack your money until you reach your goals. If you put some money up and come back to it a few hours later, that's not saving. Saving this shit takes time and patience. It's hard, but the payoff is worth it."

She stared deep into my eyes for a long time before finally handing me my bread. I was so happy I don't remember eating my food. It got ate, though. 'Cause I was starving. The moment I was done I ran into my room and got dressed I already knew where I was gonna go and what I was gonna do when I got there.

There was a Radio Shack downtown that had a double deck boombox I wanted. It was raw! I wanted it because I could play an instrumental on one tape while recording my vocals on another. When Mike-Mike holla'd at me bout rapping and investing my cheese, it planted a seed that I immediately watered...

CHAPTER

FIVE

"Tramp traffic has been at an all time high..."
-Mac Dre

As I got older and deeper in the Game I travelled across the country and back. 'Hood to 'hood, I met real niggaz and fake ones. Popped pills with bad bitches as well as ratchet ones. Other than all the different accents and swaggers, most ghettos across America are the same. If you're really born and raised in a specific turf, your block is just an extension of your home. That's how the North Pole is to a real Crestsider.

Like I said, after eating and getting cleaned up I hit the pavement running. I was on top of the world. My only dilemma was my shoes. My brand new Addidas were ripped. There was a big-ass hole in the left one. It reminded me of what took place the night before. The sound of the shots filled my head, but I pushed 'em out as fast as they came. Still, thinking about McGraw calling me a nigger and busting that pistol at me had me hot. But, what could I do? It was the reality of the life I was born into.

Anyways, I was mad about my shoes, but I had money in my pocket so I was cool. I had two directives that morning. The first one was to get a pair of shoes. There were some red and white Nike Airs I was looking at a few weeks earlier. They were at the Foot Locker at the mall. The second mission was buying a boombox. The Radio Shack at the mall had a Zenith boombox with two decks. I had to get it 'cause I had a plan.

I really knew it was gonna be a good day when the bus came as soon as I got to the bus stop. The previous day's rain was forgotten. The sun was bright. When I got to the mall I went straight to Foot Locker. They didn't have the red and white Nikes I wanted. But, they did have some black and red Air Max's, though. I slid them on quick, threw the Addidas away and walked out the store stuntin'. My next stop was the electronics store.

As soon as I got there I saw what I was looking for. The radio was on a shelf in the middle of the store. There were other portable radios there, but none like that one. It had two 8" subwoofers in it and some tweeters too. The most important aspect of it was the two tape decks. I could start recording some tracks when I got ready. By the time I left the Radio Shack I left with a bag of blank tapes and twelve brand new Double D batteries.

You couldn't tell me nothing when I walked out that mall that morning. My shoes were flawless and my radio was booming. After buying the boombox I had enough left to buy a Eric B and Rakim tape from Tower Records. It made it into my tape deck before I stepped out the store. The sound from the speakers were crispy. The base was thick, too. In my eyes, I won.

When I got on the bus the driver pointed to a sign that said 'No Loud Music.' I scoffed at that shit even though I knew I wouldn't test 'im. That specific bus driver was notorious for kicking Cuddies off the bus on the farthest side of the city. Since I wasn't trying to run up the miles on my new Air Max's I had to respect his gangsta.

On my way down the aisle towards the back of the bus I made eye contact with a brown skinned breezy. She looked like she was in her early twenties. She kept staring at ya' boy even after I took a seat in the back row.

I ain't gonna lie. Baby was looking right. I'm not gonna take anything from her. But, again, I gotta remind you that crack hit the Bay extra hard in the 80's. It probably hit us harder than any other spot in the country. At least, that's how it felt like to me.

The reason I'm mentioning this is because I was a young street nigga who kept my feet on the pavement. I was trained to recognize the signs of a smoker. Little momma was a smoker.

The bus wasn't in motion for long before she turned towards me and said, "That's a nice radio."

"Thanks. I just got this mothafucka'."

There was a moment of silence as she looked me up and down. Then she asked what my name was.

"Dre."

"I'm Rene. I think I seen you before."

"I'm from the Crest."

"So am I. Hold-up... Ain't you Peeda Weeda's nephew? You stay on Cynthia Way, huh?"

"Yeah. How you know?"

"I'm from the Crest, too, nigga!" she looked around suspiciously then asked, "You working?"

I still had one of the rocks the cuddies gave the day before. "Yeah, I got a pack. What's up? You want some?"

Even before the sentence left my mouth, my mind was already heading to a back room. See, back then, the easiest thing to get with a rock was some pussy, or some head. The cuddies were on that shit. If you got caught tricking with a smoker you'd get roasted something decent, though. Still, we all did it every we got.

My mind was on her behind and apparently, she was on the same tip because she got up out of her seat and took the one next to me. Before I knew what she was doing, she leaned in and put her tongue in my ear. On God, that shit made my dick hard immediately!

"You ever had a girl tickle the head of your dick with her tonsils?"

"Naw," I smiled. "But I'd like to try it."

"Then, you need to come with me once we get to the Crest."

"You ain't gotta tell me twice!"

As soon as we got to the Crest we stepped off the bus and started strolling towards Kemper Street. That's where she told me she lived with her parents. I had my radio on full blast, beating up the block like I was in a car with twelves. I was really feeling myself that morning.

We had to enter her house from the side door. She told me she had left it unlocked before leaving that morning. Her family wouldn't let her have a key. She didn't tell me that part, but it was obvious. She was obviously on drugs so she most likely burnt her bridges while chasing that coke cloud. Regardless of how we ended up getting inside, she told me her parents wouldn't be home 'til after six p.m. That's all that mattered to me.

It was a typical turf house. Two car garage, living room, den and kitchen on the first floor. Three bedrooms on the second floor. It didn't look like her family was rich, yet they didn't seem to want for nothing, either.

She took me upstairs and left me in her bedroom while she went to the bathroom. Her room didn't look lived in at all. It just seemed plain Jane as if she really hadn't spent that much time in it.

After setting my radio down in the corner I climbed on her bed and got comfortable. When she came back in she looked refreshed. With a bright smile on her face she said, "So what's up? You ready?"

I sat up quick. "Hell yeah!"

"You got a rock?"

"I already told you I gotchu."

"Let me get it, then. I'm gonna blow your mind! Let me get one right now so I can take a hit to get me in the mood. I won't even smoke the whole thing right now. I just need a wake up."

You know what, y'all. Baby could've told me anything at that point. I was already eyeing her lips, titties and hips. She had a short pony tail, but her hair was silky. It wasn't like she was a smelly, bald-headed street walking crack head. She actually looked good, so I was trying to hit that in the worst way.

I gave her my last stone. She tossed it in her mouth then spit it back out a few seconds later. The difference was now there were two white pebbles instead of one. Next, she reached under her bed and took out a shoebox.

She reached inside and took out a can she had made into a pipe. It had cigarette ashes in it for a filter, too.

Baby put one of the rocks on the can than went to the window, opened it and took a seat on the ledge. After flicking her lighter and putting the flame to the crackling cream she took a hit, held it in for a long time then blew out a large plume of thick white smoke.

I'll never forget the smell of crack smoke. The first half of my life was spent selling rocks. That particular scent was always in the air. The 'hood was so turnt' up that sometimes you could smell it in a passing breeze.

It seemed as if that was all she needed. After blowing out the smoke, she came over to the side of the bed I was closest to. Her pupils were dilated and a little glossy, too.

"You ready?" she asked.

That's the only coaxing I needed. I reached straight for her skirt and unzipped the side of it. My heart started racing as it dropped to her feet. Her panties were sexy-as-fuck! They were small and blue with a red bow on the front.

She kicked her shoes off and did a little twirl to show me what she was working with. I'm telling you right now, I'm an ass man. I'm all about fat asses! Rene's cheeks were barely contained in them tight cotton panties.

My eyes were parked on her coochie when she took her button-up off and tossed it on top of her skirt. When I looked up, I was like: "That's wazzup!" Her bra matched her panties, and just like her ass, they were spilling out the cups.

I snatched my shirt off real quick. Then, as I was about to snatch my pants off I remembered I had that pistol that I found the night before in my back pocket. I pulled it out and set it on the dresser. Then I took my pants off. But, I'm a fly nigga so I took a second to fold my shit.

Everything, including my gun went next to my shoes and my radio. I wasn't bout to wrinkle my shit up since I didn't know what the rest of the day would bring. When it was all said and done, I was standing next to her in my boxers with a mushroom poking out.

"Damn, boy! Your young-ass is working with something, ain't you!"

My smile was filled with pride. If there's one thing I've always had it's a long, hard, thick dick.

"Yeah, I got swipe," I told her. "But I'm trying to see what you working with."

She blushed before reaching behind herself and unclasping her bra. My eyes must've betrayed my lust because she started laughing when she saw my expression after her bra came off. I didn't care, though. She had some juicy melons. They were brown with dark colored nipples. Smoker, or not, baby was sexy!

I went straight to 'em! Ya' boy attacked them titties. I put my lips on them like they was candy. Even though I was young, my sexual wisdom was sophisticated. Where other Cuddies my age were ignorant to the needs of women, I wasn't. I knew I needed to make my mark in the dark. Not only did I know my job was to please any woman who welcomed my One-Eyed Willy. I was actually kinda skillful at it.

My lips sucked on her nips till her areolas stretched. I started playing with her. I'd let it go a little then I'd nibble on it some more. When I looked up at her, I saw her eyes closed as she let out a lustful moan. That's when I knew I was on my shit! I switched tits and did it again. This time,

I flicked her gumdrops with my tongue while sucking on 'em. By the look on her face, she was loving every moment of it.

After a few minutes of getting lost in her chest she pushed me away so she could slide her panties off.

Damn, y'all! That nappy-dugout was fat-as-fuck!

She had a hairy pussy with thick lips, just like I loved them. Her clit was thick, too. It stuck out from in between her lips. Her pussy looked like a Sonic Burger; the lips were the bread, the clit was the meat.

Mmmm-mmm-mm!

She pulled me back towards her. I sat down next to her and slid my right hand between her legs. At first, I slid one finger into her wet pussy. The slickness of her crevice was silky. It smelled clean, too.

Again, after a few minutes, she switched gears. She turned her whole body towards me and started kissing me. I'm gonna keep it gutta with y'all; usually, I wouldn't put my tongue in the mouth of any bitch, let alone, a smoker. But, Rene had me on one. Maybe it was the fact that she was pretty and smelled clean. Maybe it was the setting. The fact that we were in a nice house and all that kinda made it feel normal. We leaned back and she started tugging at my boxers. Next thing I knew, I was butt-ass naked. Our make-out session turnt' up real quick. Our tongues met, wrestled and circled each other. I slid a second finger inside of her, pushing them in as deep as I could.

"Mhmm," she moaned. "I need that dick, Dre."

By then, my snake was ready to strike. It was twitching and hopping around. Spitting precum, ready to head-butt something. I slid on top of her. She slid her legs open invitingly. Then she took ahold of my slithering serpent and slid it into her slick slit. That pussy was so silky-smooth, it almost got me to lose my cool. My goal was to take my time with her. But baby wrapped her legs around me, taking that option away real quick.

Baby was a beast. She did some shit I hadn't experienced yet. Rene had a snapper! She squeezed my dick with her pussy muscles while pulling me towards her with her legs. The resistance brought a beautiful struggle to the table.

I was balls deep in her when we started kissing again. With a little tuning we found our rhythm. In and out, in and out...

I stroked that pussy faster and faster as each moment that passed by. The bed springs were screaming after a while. The headboard was pounding against the wall like an irate inmate kicking on his cell door.

The bottom line was Rene had some good pussy. She was so wet the swipe was sliding in and out of her indiscriminately. To get a better handle of things I reached beneath her and gripped her ass cheeks. One in each hand. I used them as handles to pull her towards me as I drilled the dugout.

As far as fuck-faces went, we were exchanging some ugly ones. Rene looked determined when she looked in my eyes and demanded, "Beat this pussy up, Dre! Do your shit, cuddy! Oh shit!" she yelled.

I was going a hundred miles an hour in that pussy. The Jackhammer was on a mission to destroy some shit. After a steady twenty minutes of pounding that pussy I felt her body tighten up. I was kissing her when she squealed out of nowhere.

"Fuuuck!" she yelled.

She started shaking uncontrollably! I tried to slam this stick up in her even deeper. But I couldn't pull it all the way out for the dive 'cause she had her legs wrapped around me so tight I couldn't move. It felt like I was in a serious wrestling match. I was trying to drill harder, but the struggle was real. Her sex-fueled leg lock had my thrusts drastically restricted.

Then it was my body that reacted. My nuts constricted then exploded. I came harder and longer than I ever had before that day! Waves of lust electrified my nerves, sucking all my energy out in the explosion of cum.

A lesser man would've gotten sidetracked by that pussy's tug-of-war. But not me. I had to go. I couldn't wait to get home with my new radio and bag of blank tapes. After pulling up out the pussy I went to the bathroom; washed my nuts in the sink and got dressed.

I'll never forget that sexy smoker. As I walked away from her house that day I looked back and saw a thick plume of coke coming from her bedroom window.

The energy from the day had me floating in my Air Max's. I had the radio blasting 106.1 KMEL. There was a whole plan formulating in my head. I was gonna get the Cuddies to sit down and write some shit. Then we'd record some tapes and sell 'em at school. I was gonna take over the rap game. I just knew it.

As I look back on that day, I realize how naive I'd been. The music industry is deep and can get complicated at times. But I had drive and determination. In my head, failure wasn't an option. My mind was made up. I was gonna make my millions in the rap game.

A while later, I turned onto my street and saw something that immediately ruined my day. Officer McGraw was standing outside my house talking to my momma. His cop car was on the curb menacingly posted up. My first instinct was to walk on by. But, that didn't work. My radio gave me away.

The moment I hit the block he looked in my direction. We made eye contact and it was on. He yelled, "Hicks! Get over here!"

My mommma called out, "Dre!"

I was like, *Fuck dat!* I made an about face and took off in the direction I came from. In theory, I should've gotten away easier then than the night before. He was further away from me this time around. The problem was I had the boom box in my hand. Not only did I not wanna lose it; I couldn't risk breaking it, either. On top of that, in my panic to protect the Zenith I totally forgot the pistol parked in the back pocket of my jeans!

I couldn't have covered twenty yards before another police cruiser pulled onto the street heading in my direction. "Fuck!" I muttered. Jamal was in the back seat. They had the Cuddy and now they were coming for me!

The only chance I had was cutting through a yard and hitting some fences. It was hard to do. But I dropped the radio and took off towards the cut. Years later, I saw some videos of some guys in Chicago doing Parkour and it reminded me of that day. I was running through backyards, hopping and climbing fences like it was an obstacle course.

I just knew I was gonna get away that day. My adrenaline was pumping so hard. If it would've been one or two punk police chasing me, it would've most likely been a replay of the previous night. The problem was McGraw wasn't solo this time. I hit the last fence and found myself stuck because I was surrounded. Not only was McGraw behind me on foot, but when I hit the street I was suddenly facing two different cop cars. Each one of them already had a Cuddy in the back.

I must've paused like a deer in some headlights because I saw Coolio trying to yell something at me. A second later, BAM! McGraw tackled me from behind.

Damn...

It took four punk-police to drag me kicking and screaming into the backseat of that cop car. I was hot! The Solano County Juvenile Hall was in Fairfield, the next city over in the county I lived in. They took all four of us to the Hall's that day. We were charged with burglary, evading arrest, and stealing a car.

Oh... and I got charged with a concealed weapon.

I never saw that boom box again...

CHAPTER SIX

"Me and my team, we a machine.
You fuck with my man, I'ma have to intervene..."
-Mac Dre

Three years later...

High school was a place and a time where I really got known. The streets had given me and the louies wisdom beyond our years. So we really shined during that time. We kept that bitch lit everyday of the week.

I went to Hogan High. Just like any other high school in the Bay, you had to come fly, or don't come at all. Everyday was like a video shoot. Since me and my team stayed getting our two's and fews any which way we knew how, we all stayed clean. Brand new kicks with a fresh fit was mandatory. That's how you stayed with some tail in ya' face.

After the high-speed through the turf, McGraw and his cronies took us to Juvenile Hall. I still remember the address: 2010 West Texas Street...

We all did a little time in that bitch at one point or another. For that situation, Kilo Curt did the most time. They gave him six months at a boys ranch. The rest of us did a few months in the halls and got out early.

We stayed going in and out of juvie throughout teenage years. For some of us, the counselors in there were damn near the closest thing we had to fathers. Mr. C, Jay, Ingram and Mr. Wilson damn near raised half the Crest.

Still, despite our juvenile delinquencies most of us stayed in school. To tell you the truth, I stayed in school for the girls. And, 'cause there really wasn't much else for me to do other than hang out on the turf all day.

Don't get me wrong, the Crest was poppin'. But the hood wasn't the only spot in the V that was turnt' all the way up. There's a hood called Millersville; it's the next closest turf to ours. There's the Waterfront, which is Central Vallejo. West Vallejo do they thang too. Then, there's the South which is called Hillside...

The North Pole and the South side didn't get along at the time. Of course, I'm gonna rep' my turf to the fullest, but the Hills was poppin' too. They did what they did extremely well. If you've ever heard of E-40 and The Clique, then I'm sure you're familiar with their side of town.

40 Water and his team went to Hogan too. We really didn't really fuck with each other. I didn't and him like that. But I still didn't like that nigga or any of his homies. He was a few years older than me and my cuddies. Add that in with the fact that he was from the other side and it made it to where we really didn't push in the same circles.

Me and the louies actually got into a few incidents with them fools over the years. Later, after I got out of prison, I started fucking with 40 and them. But I'll tell you 'bout all that when we get to that part of the story.

There was one specific incident that took place that kinda lit a spark that pushed my passion to take this music thing serious. Even though 40 Water was a senior when I was a freshman, and the nigga went off to Grambling University he was always in the "V." He'd come through in his '69 Cougar on all vacations.

To better describe the climate of the times, I gotta mention the fact that Bay Area music really started making its mark in the mid 1980's. First and foremost, I have to give shout outs to The Mac. He was a true Country Club Crest representa'. Even though bruh was young; he was before his time, and extremely gifted. He was famous in the Bay. But most people are familiar with niggaz like Too Short and MC Hammer. While they were doing their thang with bangers like *Freaky Tales* and *Can't Touch This*, all the young niggaz in the Bay were trying to follow in their footsteps. Especially since we watched Too Short and several other lyrical wonders blow up after selling their tapes out of the trunk of their cars.

During that time, most of us believed the only way to get your chips up was either playing ball, selling drugs, pimping, or doing music. Damn near every cuddy in the Crest strived to get his bars up. Over the years, some of us took it more serious than others.

The whole Romper Room believed in this movement, so we stayed on course. All of us; Kilo Curt, J-Diggs, Coolio Da Unda Dogg and the young homey, Mac Mall all shared the same dream. We weren't the only goons from the ghetto with aspirations and goals, though. 40 and his crew were on that same mission. I gotta keep it gutta; even though I hated that nigga for a while, our rivalry really pushed me to get my music up to par.

I can't recall if it was '87 or '88. But I know 40 had already graduated. His clique was already pushing their music by the time he was a senior in high school. Their main group consisted of his brother, D-Shot; sister, Suga T; and their homey, B Legit.

I remember when 40 graduated because the Cuddies were recording hella content that summer. By the time the school year started, we all had mix tapes floating around. Rompilations were the soundtrack to the whole city, all year and every year after that.

One day in the spring of '87 or '88 we were getting out of school and that nigga was outside. 40 had a clean-ass P-nut butter brown, old school Cougar on

triple gold D's. They were out there, in front of Hogan High posted up next to his muscle car with the trunk open passing out tapes of their music.

Like I said earlier, our crews didn't get along. On some real shit, I didn't like that fat-ass nigga on a personal level. He always acted like he was better than everybody else. On top of that, he was from the other side so it was inevitable that we bump heads.

It was after school and I was walking with Coolio and Jay when I saw them niggaz. I wasn't gonna stop until I heard someone call out, "Hey, sahob! Check it out!"

I just knew that whoever it was yelling, wasn't calling for me or any of the louies 'cause *sahob* is a Hillside thing. In the Crest we call each other cuddy.

Sahob is what they called each other on the Hillside. So, there was no way whoever was yelling was talking to me. At least, that's what I thought. But when I recognized 40's voice say, "Dre! I know you hear me, ya' little whippa snappa!" I knew they was talking to us.

Jay looked at me and scoffed. Then he asked, "What dat nigga want, cuddy?"

"Man, fuck dat nigga!" Coolio said.

"My sentiments exactly. But we still gotta see what the fuck he talking 'bout," I told them.

Then all three of us crossed the street towards a small crowd that gathered around the Cougar. Mall caught up with us on the walk across the street. Niether one of knew what we were about to get into, but we were ready for whatever.

When we reached them, Jay asked, "What y'all want?"

It was four cuddies and four Hillside niggaz. The tension was in the air and it couldn't be ignored.

Even before we started talking, a crowd of instigators started forming. School was letting out so the block was filled with people. Everybody just knew something tricky was bout to go down. It was a magnate for nosy niggaz and messy bitches.

The Crest was deep at a Hogan High. But I'm not gonna sit here and tell you the Cutthroat Committee was mobbin' up that day 'cause it wasn't like that right then and there. It was just me, Coolio, Jay and Mall. If anything, 40 had just as many supporters as we did.

Earl aka E-40 answered Jay: "I just came through to bless the chubbies with a tape or two of this Game we spittin'-"

"Chubbies!?" spat Coolio. "Nigga, you know it's Threes C's in this bitch! We cuddies, nigga!"

B Legit stepped up. He was way taller than the rest of us so he towered over Coolio. "Slow ya' role, lil nigga!"

40 stuck his arm out to stop his peoples from stepping past the scrimmage line. Not that any of us gave a fuck. yeah, they were older than us. But we were wild-as-fuck! We were trained to fight. I doubt any of the louies gave a shit if we squabbled up with them niggaz, or not.

"Slow this scene down, my weebles. We didn't come for them Mike Tyson Punch-Out scenes. I just heard the Romper Room was pushing tapes these days. I figured we could exchange some Game. Put a few verses in the air. What's up? You got some music on you?" 40 asked me specifically.

"Yeah. I stay with a Rompilation or two in the bag. Why? What's up?" I replied.

"A'ight, pimp-juice. Let's go one for one. Here you go."

He handed me a tape that was still in the plastic. The case was sealed like it came straight out of Tower Records. It had a real cover, too. It was a picture of 40 with his crew. I gave him one of mine, and from the gate anyone watching would've seen the difference. My tape was in a case, but all it had on it was *Romper Room mix Volume 3,* written in marker.

40 took the tape I handed him and tossed it to his cute-ass sister, Sugar T. "Put dat-dere in the deck, Suga'. But, first play some of our shit."

"A'ight, 40," she replied.

Suga' pressed play and the trunk started rumbling! 40 had major beat in that bitch. I ain't gonna lie, his music was raw. It was clear too. He definitely had access to studio time. All his shit had the quality sound of being mixed and mastered.

40's word play along with his story telling finesse was shitting on my work at that time. As soon as I heard his work, I knew my mix tape wasn't gonna shine as bright next to it. My handicap was all my music was recorded on a boom box. We also had a Casio keyboard we used for beats. Regardless, the Rompilations were raw. But it wasn't at the level of music that was mixed and mastered inside of a studio.

They played a track off the Clique's first album and the crowd of onlookers went crazy. Niggaz was cheering and all kinds of shit.

"Yeah," 40 began. "We been in the lab percolating some real musical mixtures. When y'all don't see me, I'm at Grambling perfecting the art of story telling. Y'all know how the H-I-Double L side do it." Then he slid the spotlight on me. "Where you at, Dre? Where's ya' poetry, young blood? Which track you wanna toss out 'dere?"

"Play the first song on the A-side. It's some real Louie shit," I told 'im. But D-Shot was on some bullshit.

Before 40 could say anything, D-Shot called out to Suga T and said, "Play anything on the B side."

That move right there made me wanna slap the taste outta that nigga! I saw the anger in the Cuddie's eyes, too. I already knew it was gonna be some shit once he did that. It didn't matter, though. The hyenas were itching for a fight.

A few moments later, the music started. 40 had a top of the line music system. He had tweeters, mids and lows wired up right. Which is cool, but not if you didn't record your music in a studio.

As soon as the Rompilation started, I could hear the background noise. But Suga T must've fucked with the EQ 'cause it quickly cleared up a little. Then my voice came on. The verse was raw. It was a true story of how me and the louies had ran a train on a ripper. It was actually sounding hard for a second. I thought we was gonna win that pissin' contest for a minute.

But then the punk-bitch did some fuck-shit! After about thirty seconds of my music beating up the Cougar's trunk, Suga T cut it off and tossed my tape out the window.

"Man, get that shit up outta here!" she scoffed from the front seat of the muscle car.

Coolio was the first Cuddy to react to that disrespectful shit. "What, bitch?!"

He broke through the crowd and started towards her. She was getting out the car, too. She was cocky, like she wanted that smoke!

40 and his peoples weren't 'bout to let anyone just dog her out, though. They grouped up, creating a scrimmage line with 40 at the helm. They blocked the Unda Dogg's path. And we all reacted, getting ready for a stomp out convention.

"Hold-up, sahob!" 40 said. "That's my lil sister you talking to. You need to show a more 'spect than that!"

"Fuck dat!" Jay shouted. "She disrespected the cuddy's music!"

Jay Diggs was known for his hands. All the cuddies could squabble up, but Jay had KO's on top of KO's under his belt. Not only could he hold his own, he couldn't stand cats from the South. Yeah, 40 and his cipher were older than us. But we didn't give a fuck 'bout all that. Especially not Diggs.

"Check this out," 40 started. "We on some quality control shit. We reppin' the V to the fullest. When it comes to puttin' music out, we puttin' for the "V." Y'all the one's who's dissin' the movement by puttin' this garbage out."

Then before Jay had the chance to reply, 40 turned to me and said, "Lil Dre."

"My name is Mac Dre!" I growled, ready to hit that nigga in the throat.

In the most sarcastic voice this nigga could muster, 40 said, "I see you steamin' like tug boat. A lil engine that could syndrome. But y'all ain't gotta be mad at me, the Clique or Suga T." By then, Suga T found a spot right next to him. "What I don't understand is, since you took the Mac's name and he's obviously y'all cuddy; why y'all not in the studio wit' 'im? Why y'all shit sound like it was recorded on a tape player with a keyboard beat? If the little Mac-"

"Keep the cuddy's name out ya' mouth!" Mac Mall spat like venom.

"See what I'm talkin' 'bout," continued 40. "You lil niggaz got no respect for your elders. But then again, isn't that how it goes in life? Even the Nazarenes had forsaken Jesus Christ when he spoke the truth. So I can't expect anything different from some gentiles like y'all. Either way, let me sprinkle y'all wit' some wise-domage. You niggaz go to this school everyday. Yet, neither one of y'all takin' advantage of that band room. You named yourselves after a real Game spitter. Yet, none of y'all in that studio. You obviously half-steppin' wit' this shit. But, what can we expect? Y'all from the Crest!"

That was all it took. That last remark cashed a check 40's fat-ass couldn't cash. Jay reached back and hit that nigga with the hardest right cross I had ever seen! 40 stumbled back but caught himself on the trunk of his car before he hit the ground. It immediately triggered a melee.

Everybody got to rocking. I caught D-Shot, but he was on the offensive too. Real talk, all of us started chunk'n 'em right there in the middle of the circle of onlookers. Dust was flying as an explosion of punches were exchanged between our crews!

There were people who went to our school who repped the South just like there were those in attendance who were from the Crest. It was really about to turn into a full fledged riot until someone intervened.

Mr. Jennings, the P.E. teacher started yelling over the crowd. He came running out of the front of the school with a group of teachers all yelling for everyone to stop fighting.

I wasn't about to let a few teachers stop me from getting mines. The louies were cut from that same clothe as well. So we all kept chunk'n 'em with them niggaz. But then we heard the 'hood call.

"YEE! YEE! McGraw's coming! YEE!"

Everyone scattered. Vallejo P.D. was some real bitches! That was enough to get everybody on they track star tip...

CHAPTER

SEVEN

"It's money in these streets and it can't be ignored."
-Mac Dre

I once heard someone say, "A formidable foe makes a person stronger."

The way I break that down is the harder the ops are, the deeper you gotta dig in to beat 'em. That type of shit will make anyone stronger.

Yeah, 40 and them niggaz were competition. But I didn't see them as an obstacle in the rap game. In my eyes, the real opposition was the odds of actually making it. It wasn't gonna be easy. Even though we all saw it happening with The Mac, and them Hillside niggaz, everyone knew it wasn't as easy as it looked.

I'll never forget that day we got into it with them niggaz. It really was the catalyst that motivated me and the cuddies to push for stardom. For a minute, after hittin' a few fences to get away from McGraw, we all walked in silence. It was a beautiful day. But the gang was hot! 40 had been high siding on the louies ever since we started going to Hogan High.

Even though he wasn't even at the school with us anymore, he was still showing up and starting shit.

It was Coolio who broke the silence first when he said, "Hey, Dre. Don't let them bitch-ass niggaz get up under your skin."

"I ain't tripping off that fat-ass nigga. His sister just hating 'cause a nigga won't give her no play."

"You right," agreed Jay. "But, cuddy, keeping it all the way gutta; we gotta step our game up. Fuck them niggaz. It's on sight when I see any of them suckaz. But, they shit was on point. They music had a whole different sound than the tapes we been making."

"I heard it," I said. "But, what do you expect? Them niggaz really be in the studio."

Then Mall spoke up, "My relly says they fucking with Little D from 6-9 Ville in Oakland. That's whose really bank-rollin' everything 40 and them niggaz been doing."

We all knew who Little D was. He was about our age, but the nigga was a millionaire. He was a 'hood legend who got rich at a young age by selling crack.

At that time, no one in my immediate circle was rich. We didn't know Little D personally. Even if we did, we weren't set up to push the type of weight they were moving. 40's team knew him and they were eating with him. It wasn't a secret. What we didn't know at the time was the rap game was really just a front for the dope game. Yeah, 40 and his team did know him and were doing their shit with the music. Yet, what they were really doing was cleaning D's money along with their own.

"It takes money to make money," Coolio stated. "For real. If we ever wanna make it in the game, we need some money, y'all."

"You right," I agreed. "I ain't gonna lie; You seen them tape covers they had? They shit looked like it came straight out the store."

"They are in the stores," Jay commented.

We had reached the Crest by then. Being in the 'hood seemed to lighten the mood, 'cause the cloud of the recent skirmish was already forgotten. We hit the Crest Park and posted up under a gazebo.

"Well, it looks like we need to come up with some bread," I said. "More than what we've already been getting."

"We need a million dollar plan," Jay said.

"Exactly," I agreed.

Something I always loved about the louies is once we put our minds together we can't be stopped. Niggaz get to brainstorming like we're a creative team for a Fortune 500 company.

"Getting money is mandatory," Coolio added. "But, what's the goal? We gotta have specifics."

That was on me. I had been thinking about all that shit for a minute. So, I had a lot to say on the subject.

"This is what I was thinking," I started. "We gonna need some studio time. And that shit cost. There's a studio in Frisco where we can get ten hour blocks for five bills. I saw an ad in a *Word Up Magazine*. There's a company that prints up tape covers and fliers just like what 40 and them niggaz got. The best package was like two thousand."

"Damn, cuddy. That's some bread!" Mall said.

"I know," I replied. "And, it ain't all we need, either. The beats cost money. If we gonna be in the studio we gonna have to have better beats. I don't know how much beats cost, but they do."

Silence.

I think all of us had money on our mind. All of us sold cream in the 'hood. It always gave us enough for everything we needed. But it wasn't gonna get us the type of bread we really wanted.

"So how we gonna get this money?" Coolio asked.

"Why don't we hit some houses?" Jay asked. "Y'all remember when Chris Peeler found that safe with ten G's in it? If we really go on one, we can do this. We just gotta all agree to put our money together."

"Yeah," Mall chimed in. "Chris got his 'Vette like that. But-"

"But, nothing!" I said before he could inject some bad juju in the mix. "We all know flockin' is hit or miss. You miss more than you hit. But, when you hit, the payoff is fat. What if we go out of town? If we go to Napa and hit some of them white folks with they chips up? We might hit the jackpot!"

"He's right," Coolio agreed. "This some real Romper Room shit. We can go to Napa and fuck 'em up. What y'all think?"

"We wit' it," we all said.

"A'ight..." I told them. "We can start tomorrow. Somebody gotta holla at Kilo. We can meet up in the morning and ride out there and do our shit!"

After that, we all went our separate ways. The plan was set. We were gonna get our start up capital by flocking in Napa. In my eyes, the plan was realistic. Napa was a town just outside of the "V" where rich white people lived. It's known for their vineyards. They got a bunch of wineries and distilleries out there. That's where the money's at.

The fact that there were no Black people out there meant we had to be smooth. The moment we entered their city limits we'd have to be on point because we were definitely gonna stick out like wolves in a hen house. Nevertheless, the promise of possible profits were enough to get us to take that risk.

$$$$$

We all met up at Kilo Curt's house the next morning. All five of us were on a mission to get paid. Me, Jay, Coolio, Mall and Curt were in attendance, ready to embark on the day's money chase. Kilo's momma worked at the hospital so she was always gone. They had a station wagon that she would let him drive while she was at work. Kilo was on one that morning 'cause we ate breakfast at his house and he was tripping off how fast we went through the box of *Lucky Charms* his mom had just bought him.

We hung out at the cuddy's house until about nine. Then we bounced. By 9:25 we were pulling up to the outskirts of Napa. It was really different than Vallejo. In the "V" everything is congested. Out there, all the homes were big and spread out. Our target area was the outskirts of the city where the homes all had vineyards. Those were the ones where the millionaires lived in. At least, that's what we all assumed, which wasn't too far off from the truth.

It took us awhile before we found the right spot. The property was hella-hella big. They had a lot of trees all around it, with two houses right next to one another. Even though the houses stood next to one another, they each had they own driveways. And they were separated by a wall of bushes and trees.

There were at least ten acres of vineyards surrounding each property. It was perfect. We could hit one house then go straight to the next one. All I could think was hopefully one of 'em would have the treasure chest we were all searching for. Curt drove the station wagon up about a half mile away from the houses and parked. It was a wooded area with trees and all kinds of greenery so we easily found a spot in the cuts that hid our ride from the road.

In the movies, burglars usually break into houses at night while the inhabitants are in bed asleep. Cat burglars creeping through shit while someone's dead to the world. That does happen, but that's some dangerous shit. We hit houses in the daylight hours 'cause that's when most people are at work. That way you don't gotta worry about being quiet and having to tip toe around. On top of that, you can take your time in the spot you're hitting when you know it's empty. Not to mention the fact that you can get yourself killed by breaking into a house when someone's inside.

Once we got situated we hit the woods running. We already knew what house we were gonna run up in first. There was a blue and grey house as well as a green and brown one. Since the green and brown house was two storys we decided to hit that one second.

The coast was clear when we crept up on the first house. It had a two car garage that wasn't connected to the main house. The rest of the property seemed empty. No cars, no dogs. Nothing. It also had manicured shrubs surrounding it. This let us know even though things were quiet, someone definitely lived there.

For some reason, I just assumed it was a lawyer or something who lived there. I don't know why I was thinking that, but I do remember it passing through my mind.

Mall and Curt went around the left side of the house, behind some bushes. Me and Coolio took the opposite route. Jay posted up at the edge of the property. He was our look-out while we did our thang.

Coolio and I took our time as we circled the house. We peeked inside the windows to make sure the house was empty. The inside looked clean, and the furniture seemed expensive. It seemed as if we were on the right track.

When we reached the back of the house we met up with the cuddies.

"Coolio," Curt said. "It's on you."

"What's up, y'all? You found a way in?" Coolio asked.

"Yup! It's the kitchen window. It's open. C'mon, let me show you."

We followed Curt and Mall to the opening they found. Just like they said, it was wide open. After taking the screen off, we gave Coolio a boost. After that, we were all inside in less than a minute.

The interior of the home was nice. The layout of that house was raw. There were three bedrooms altogether. They were located on one end of the house. The living room, kitchen and den were in the center of the whole setup. The far end of the house had another room and a side door that led outside between the house and the garage. The floors were Spanish Tile. All the kitchen appliances looked new and expensive. Exactly what I expected when we first planned the licks the day before.

The plan was always the same. We split up. Each of us took different rooms. Somehow, I ended up in a kid's bedroom. It looked like a teenage girl's room. Different sorts of gel and hairsprays were all over the dresser. But the main tell tail sign that I was in a teen's room was the mirror on the dresser. It was covered with a bunch of pictures of other teens.

It didn't take me long to realize she didn't have shit. So I moved on to the next room. There was a home office next to the teen's room. I found a computer which was worth a lot back then. The problem was that a computer doesn't fit in my pocket. We had strict rules against that shit so I ignored it. A few minutes later, as I was rummaging through a file cabinet I suddenly heard Curt yelling from another room a lil deeper in the house.

"I hit! I hit, cuddy! C'mon, y'all!"

His voice was music to my ears. A platinum album to be exact. After taking a look in the closet of the room I was in I went to go see what Kilo Curt was talking about.

The louies all heard 'im yelling too. We all found him at the same time. He was looking hyped as hell! He was standing in the center of the room holding a handful of gold. The room wasn't a bedroom. There were three sewing machines set up against the far wall. There was also a table set against another wall with two mink coats carefully laid next to one another. On the same table there were several diamond bracelets and some heavy rings. They were all perfectly displayed on a soft jewelry cloth.

"Dayum!" Mall said.

"Jackpot!" Coolio exclaimed.

I picked up one of the bracelets and put it on my wrist. "How much you think this shit worth?"

"I don't know," Curt replied. "Let's pack this shit up. We can find all'at out later."

"Did y'all find anything else?" Mall asked.

"Naw," Coolio and I replied. We weren't trippin', though. The jewels we found in that room was the treasure chest we had all been looking for.

While everyone else was grabbing something, I said, "We need to take this shit to Jay. By the time he tucks it, we'll be halfway done with the next house."

Coolio held up a mink coat and said, "Dre, how much you think this worth?"

"I don't know, cuddy. Probably five to fifty G's a piece. Minks are worth some shit. I heard Chinchilla minks cost fifty! Either way, somebody gonna know somethin' when we get back to the Crest."

"I know that's right!" agreed Mall and Curt.

After cuffing the loot we slid out the back door. Mall ended up staying with Jay so he could help him with all the stuff we took. It was too much for him to take on by himself. Plus, we wanted to take care of the minks since that was what we thought was the real meal tickets. Me, Coolio and Curt went to the next house...

CHAPTER EIGHT

"Can you hear me now?"
-Mac Dre

When we reached the next house the vibe was just as still as the last one. There was a brand new black on black Volvo in the driveway. But other than that, the spot looked empty. Nevertheless, we scoped the scene. After peeking in the windows and not seeing anyone we knew we could go inside.

The house was easier to get into than the last one. The garage door was open, so was the one that led to the interior of the home from the inside of the garage. Something you learn while flocking is a lot of people tend to leave their doors open. This is especially so for white folks who live in the suburbs. I guess they think since they don't live in crime infested neighborhoods there's no need for all that. That's why we always check the door knobs and windows before bashing our way into a juxt.

The layout of the second house was different than the first one. It was two stories. The lower level didn't have any bedrooms. There was a living room, den, game room and kitchen.

In the living room there was a big screen TV set to a country music channel. Somehow, the sound system was connected to the whole house. Every room had the sound of country music coming out of some hidden speakers.

The home's surround sound system caught my attention because the stereo system was top of the line. At the time, I was recording my tapes on a cheap set up. I knew I could do more with what was in that house. The problem was it went against the rule we set ages earlier: Never take anything that doesn't fit in your pockets. Every time a Cuddy broke that law, something always seemed to go wrong.

The more I thought about it; taking that stereo system started seeming like a viable option. I started to reason with myself that the reason the rule was enacted in the first place was because the chances of people seeing you carry shit away from the house you were robbing got higher if you were walking up the street carting a big items like couches and refrigerators. The thing about the house we were in at the time was that it was located on a secluded property. No one knew how much time we had, but it was obvious no one was around to see what we were doing.

"Dre!" Coolio called out from a few feet away. "Let's go upstairs."

Before I continue I gotta tell y'all we were all excited from the win we caught at the previous house. Add that in with the fact that we were out in the boondocks, with no one in sight and our security consciousness was at an all time low. We were moving through this house without a care in the world.

The layout of the second floor was typical. At the top of the stairs there were three bedrooms; two to the left, one to the right. A full bathroom sat directly across from the top of the staircase. I was the first one to reach the top of the stairs. Without thinking, I cut to the right. It seemed like the best choice, since I assumed it was the master bedroom.

The door was shut. I could hear some country music coming from behind it. Under normal circumstances it would've raised red flags immediately. But the whole house was hooked up to the same system so I didn't think anything of it. I grabbed the doorknob, twisted it and barged into the room like I lived there.

"Oh shit!!!"

I knew I had fucked up the moment I set foot in that room. The first thing I saw was a fat, nasty, four hundred pound, naked white lady seated at the edge of a king-sized bed. Her body was facing the door so I saw everything she had to offer. She was leaning back resting her weight on her elbows. Her gigantic titties were hanging on both sides of her body. She had roles on top of roles on her stomach and her legs were cocked up like some TV antennas. There was a skinny-ass, little white dude kneeling on the floor between her legs. He was holding her humungous thighs up while he went crazy at her all you can eat buffet.

As I think about it now, that shit was funny. He was licking that pussy like a real sea food lover. Like I said, now it's funny. But, when it happened, I got hit with the thickest shot of adrenaline I could remember ever having. I knew I fucked up.

First, the fat lady looked at me. Then, the man stopped feasting and turned around to see what his bitch was staring at.

I was in shock. For real! I know this is cliché to say, but on everything I love, I must've looked like I got caught with my hand in the proverbial cookie jar. Next thing I know, I felt one of the cuddies run up behind me.

"Awe, fuck!" one of the cuddies exclaimed.

Suddenly, the man hopped up and yelled, "What-da-god-dayum!"

Even after the naked white man hoped up, his date stayed in the same position. She was holding her legs up with a big-ass pussy wide open for the world to see.

"Hot-doggy!" the white man yelled. "I'm gonna kill you fuckin' thieving niggers!"

He ran straight towards his closet! We all knew what that meant. I quickly turned around, along with the rest of the louies and we took off running down that flight of stairs. We took off like our lives depended on it. Down the stairs, through the living room, and straight through the first door we found that led outside.

"BOOM! BOOM! BOOM!"

Shotgun blasts went off behind us. I saw Jay hiding behind some bushes when someone yelled, "Run!"

Don't ask me why, but I had to look back. The skinny white dude was out there, butt-ass naked busting a double barreled shotty at me and the cuddies! We all smashed straight through some bushes. When we got to the station wagon, everyone hopped in and Jay sped away, leaving a cloud of dust in our wake.

I damn near shitted on myself when Yosemite Sam caught us in his shit. We were all living a fast and crazy life, though. Near death experiences were fucked up, but Romper Room niggaz bounced back fast from situations like that.

By the time we got back to the "V" it was just after twelve in the afternoon. The traffic was thick. And the mood was celebratory since we hit on two minks and hella jewlery.

There was a pawn shop downtown called Lincoln Pawn Shop. It was on Georgia Street. All the cuddies fucked with it 'cause the Mexican who owned it never asked questions about where we got our shit.

"Hey! Hey!" he greeted us when we came in. No one else was in his shop at the time. That was a plus in my eyes. "How's my Young cuddies these days?"

"We good, Mr. G," we all said.

"What'chu got for me today, fellas?"

Me and Mall had the minks. Jay and Coolio laid the jewelry out on the glass display counters. I'm telling you, our presentation was spectacular. On the ride back to the "V" we all started speculating on how much bread we'd get for the loot we took. In our eyes, we hit the lick of the century. It was something to be proud of. The pride in our push was apparent in our presentation.

"Check this out," Kilo told Mr. G.

"Aye, dios mio!" muttered the pawn shop owner. "You kids bout to get us all put in jail. Hold on a minute."

Mr. Garcia came from behind the counter, walked up to the front of the shop and flipped the *Open* sign to say *Closed*. After locking the door and coming back behind the counter he said, "This is a lot of stuff you youngsters have."

As agreed earlier, Kilo spoke for all of us when he said, "I know. And we tryn'a get every penny for what we got."

"C'mon, man... Don't do me like that, cuddies. You know I do you right every time you come in here." Mr. G made it look smooth when he took out his kit for checking gold and put it on the counter next to the jewelry.

It was a hard little rock that he would scratch any gold jewelry on, and it would show us if it was real or not. After checking the necklaces, he pulled out a small looking glass type of microscope and started studying the diamond tennis bracelet we had. We all watched closely. I think all four us were already mentally spending the money we were about to clock. Then, what he said next blew all of our minds...

"Well, young cuddies. I'm sorry to be the one to tell you this, but you got a bunch of costume jewelry."

"What?!" we muttered. "Costume, what?!"

"None of it's real, guys. Here, look at the necklaces." He held them up for us to see. "You can see where the plating just scratched off. If it was real it wouldn't have done that."

We all knew that much. I can't speak for the louies on this one, but I felt like all the air got sucked out my lungs when he told us all the jewels were fugazi.

"What about the minks?" Kilo asked.

"Yeah!" we said. "We got these minks, too."

Suddenly, we all perked up like there was a chance we could still come out on top. We were all banking on the furs being Chinchillas.

"Well, then," Mr. G told us. "Let's check them out."

He picked up the first one and looked at the tag on the inside of the breast. After studying it, he put it down then did the same thing with the other one.

I held my breath. If I'm keeping it all the way real with y'all, I think all of us were holding our breaths.

"Sorry, fellas," Mr. G said while shaking his head. "Take a look at this tag. It says: Made in China. This is one hundred percent beaver fur. These coats are worth a couple hundred a piece at the most. I can give you fifty dollars for each one."

On my momma, I can't express the level of defeat I felt as I stepped out the pawn shop. Of course we took everything with us. We had to get a second, third and fourth opinion in case he was trying to play us. But they all told us the same shit.

Everything was fake!

CHAPTER NINE

"Pimp with no Gators, Air Forces and Shell Tops..."
-Mac Dre

One thing I gotta say about the rap game, or any other hustle you invest serious energy into is there's different levels to it. You're guaranteed to take some losses on your way to the top. That's in anything. Nothing worth having ever comes easily. That's why so many people quit before they reach the pinnacle of their potential.

Since the Game is so tricky, you gotta learn and master the tricks to the trade as fast as possible. I'ma keep it real with you every time I speak. I got a lot of my wisdom from experiencing situations where I made mistakes.

Like that day me and the cuddies took that trip to Napa. If one of us would've just taken the time to think, we would've realized that whoever lived in that first house was some sort of costume designer. All the sewing machines and fabrics told us that. But none of us were really paying that much attention to our surroundings.

That specific situation taught me an important lesson about paying attention to details. You gotta be like that because the Game is serious.

Since my life started out in the trenches, paying attention to the details became a survival tactic. I've seen cuddies lose their life because they ignored certain signs.

Even though we got dumped on and didn't make a dime from that trip, we still kept flocking. We didn't let it stop our mission. Me and the louies basically became a crime wave. We hit so many houses in the surrounding cities that we ended up coming up on all kinds of shit.

As far as studio equipment was concerned, we ended up with all kinds of shit. We managed to put a small studio together in my momma's garage with a beat machine and some microphones we found in a house. That's how I ended up putting out some of my rawest mixtapes.

Preparation and persistence pays off like a mothafucka! Me and the Cuddies kept the Rompilations coming. It got to the point where people from all over the "V" started coming through the Crest just to buy our music. We hadn't gotten our album covers done yet. But that didn't matter. As soon as anyone saw the three C's scribbled in marker on the tape cover they knew it was gonna be some gritty shit.

Ever since that day, we got into it with 40 and them, I was on a serious mission to make it in the music industry. All the work we had been putting in was beginning to pay off. The whole city knew Mac Dre was me and that I was on my shit. The cold thing about it was that I was still in high school. The thing about popularity and turf prestige is, although it can get you into certain circles and open up networking opportunities. Popularity alone isn't gonna get you paid.

In the back of my mind, I knew the only way I was ever gonna reach the next level of the rap game was by coming up with a nice chunk of change. Once I did that, I would have to invest it all in myself.

Everything from studio time, album covers, radio play and shows cost money. I never had an Angel Investor, so I knew there was gonna come a time when I was going to have to throw some cash at my career. That saying, It takes money to make money.

One Saturday afternoon about a year after the flocking debacle I told y'all 'bout, all the louis were posted up outside King's Market. We were just out there hanging out. Some niggaz were grindin', some were hollering at bitches. A few were playing dice between some parked cars, too. I was standing against the wall with my foot cocked up, chopping game wit' one of the cuddies when The Mac pulled up.

Again, I gotta emphasize the fact that Michael was loved by the louies. Even though he was always on the on the move, bruh stayed in contact with the turf. It was like he was conduit between our generation and the OG's who paved the way for us to kick up dust.

I'll always remember that day 'cause of the conversation we ended up having. But the smooth part came when he pulled up on us. Cuddy had a few jugs of Carlos Rossi. It was wine niggaz drank at the time. As soon he pulled up, he hopped out with some wine and red cups to share it in. This got the cuddies hyped. That, added with the fact that he was riding with a few bad bitches in the 'Lac turned the crime scene into a party machine.

It wasn't long before a whole side show started. It was a sunny day, middle of the afternoon. Suddenly people started pulling up from everywhere. Cars with beat started beating up the block. Niggaz were drinking, smoking and having a good time. That's the type of energy that came out the Crest. Especially whenever certain Cuddies showed up and showed out.

In the midst of the festivities Michael looked at me and motioned towards his car with his eyes. With a smirk on my face, I nodded and we go tin his load. He got behind the wheel. I slid into the passenger seat. This gave us some privacy to really chop Game. It had been a while since we hung out like that. And the plush leather interior of his pimped out Caddy was the perfect setting for a meeting of the minds.

"What's up wit' it, cuddy?" he asked me in his trademark smooth demeanor.

"I'm out here! Tryna do this music thang. Thanks for that plug at print shop. They got my shit looking right."

"I saw that. It's nothing, cuddy. I just love seeing the louies eating. Shiiit, I'm 'bout to go on tour with Too Short and some other niggaz out of Oakland."

"40 and them finna go wit' y'all?"

"Naw. I don't fuck with them niggaz like that."

"Fuck them niggaz."

"Well said. But, anyways... what's your next move? You know there's no time to waste out here. Every day gotta count."

I slid into the seat to get a little more comfortable. Then I said, "I need to come up on some cheese so I can get some studio time like you. This flocking shit ain't gonna last forever. It ain't even bringing in the type of revenue I really need."

"I feel you. I wish you could slide in with me, but Kyree and them be keeping shit compartmentalized. I really ain't even been in the studio after my album dropped. Lately, it's 'bout pushing this album and doing shows. But, what's good? You need some gold, or something?"

The Mac pulled out a wad of cash. He was really on his shit. It didn't matter though. I wasn't about to accept any handouts.

"Naw, cuddy. I'm not looking for anything. A nigga's just choppin' game with a real one. I'm just saying, we talkin' 'bout movin' on to the next money making mission."

"What'chu got in mind?"

"The cuddies been talking 'bout running up in shit. That ski mask game seems more profitable than burglarizing houses."

Bruh didn't reply. He just looked at me for a moment then stared out the windshield for a second. The sound of bass coming from a nearby car along with some distant laughter suddenly took center stage. He was obviously plotting on the right words to deliver. Which was cool because it let me know he was, both, listening and taking me serious. True qualities of a real homey.

"Dre, the older cuddies always emphasized the meaning behind my name. A MAC is a master at communicating. A MAC can get anything his heart desires just by opening his mouth and requesting it."

"Something like a pimp or a pastor."

"Exactly. Dre, you see how I'm always with some bad bitches when I come through? It's not 'cause I enjoy their company. Fuck no! I push with these breezies 'cause they got that pot of gold between their legs. That's money to me. And if they not willing to sell it, then I'll tell 'em what they wanna hear and they'll go get it some other way."

"Pimpin'..."

"Mac'n. It's all part of the 'ism. Playerism. Real Country Club Crest shit."

"On-my-momma!"

"Look, cuddy. I'ma holla at my big cousin and see if they can come swoop you up. These are the same niggaz that taught me the 'ism. They can lace you up real tight. I think it'll be more beneficial for you than strapping up with the louies and jackin' some shit."

"I'm wit' dat!"

"'Nuff said."

I had the cuddy drop me off at Borge's Park after that. I needed some time alone to get my thoughts together. Everyone knew the cuddy was a pimp turnt' rapper; not the other way around. He shared 'ism every time he came around.

It never crossed my mind to take that page out his book to fund my mission. But, the more I thought about it, the more it started making sense. That's what the Crest did best! The turf bred real Macs and certified players.

When I got home about an hour later, moms' told me he called and told me to be ready. That plan we had discussed earlier had to have been in full play mode. I couldn't have hid my excitement even if I wanted to. I rushed to get showered and dressed in my flyest gear. And, as soon as the sun started dipping behind the horizon I was outside waiting on the cuddies to pull up.

It was just after nine when I saw the all black Deuce and a Quarter pull up to my house. I immediately recognized the car as soon as I saw it. It belonged to Michael's older relly, Pimpin' Te. Te was a smooth talking, light skinned cuddy with a long perm and an open faced gold tooth in his mouth.

Even before the tinted window rolled down, I knew Te would be with Mac'n Louie. Louie was tall and slim. He was dark as night, and the ladies loved every inch of him. He was a pimp too. But Mac'n Lou was known in them streets for a being a beast. The cuddy had a few bodies under his belt that everybody knew about.

Just as the Buick stopped and the window came down, Louie stuck his arm out and gave me dap. "What's up wit' it, Dre? You ready for this 'ism?"

"Do a bear wipe his ass wit' a rabbit in the woods?"

Mac'n Louie smiled, "Damn right! Get in, cuddy."

I got in the back seat and was immediately taken aback by the red velour interior. That Buick was so big. It felt like I was sitting on a couch at somebody's house! The interior light bulb was red too. So when I stepped in, the vibe was illicit in all the right ways. I halfway expected some females to be in their ride, but the back seat was empty. As we pulled away, I remember thinking of how they smelled like Drakar and trees.

Expensive, sticky trees!

"What it do, young Dre?" Pimpin' Te greeted me as he looked at me through the rearview mirror, smiling so he could show off his shiny gold tooth.

"I'm blessed! Ready to soak up this 'ism y'all 'bout to lace me wit'!"

"That's what I wanted to hear, cuddy."

Mac'n Louie reached over the seat and handed me a red cup filled halfway up with brown liquor.

"Sip on this, mac. Don't drink to get drunk. Drink to get ya' tongue loose enough to spit fire in a bitch ear. This is some fifty-dollar a pint type shit. I call it gas 'cause it'll get ya' motor mouth running."

"Preach, P!" Te told him. "Give 'im dat 'ism!"

"So, where we headed?" I asked.

Pimpin' Te answered, "We 'bout to take you to one of the most poppin' blades in the State! E-1-4!"

"We going to the '0'?" I asked.

"Yeah," Mac'n Lou replied. "East Oakland. We already got some hoes ten toes down. We only came back to the turf to pick you up so we gotta get back ASAP!"

It took us just over twenty minutes to get to Oakland from Vallejo. East 14th Avenue is a street that never sleeps. It's the epicenter of hustling as far as East Oakland is concerned. You can find anything from coke to heroin to weed and/or pussy for sale on E-1-4. It's always poppin' on that Ave!

The energy on that blade was magnetic. The minute we pulled up to the parking lot where the cuddies conducted their misconduct, several different hoe bitches started running up to the Buick. The louies rolled their windows down and their hoes dropped bundles of cash in their laps.

It was the first time I ever saw an actual pimping machine in progress. Watching all them bad bitches come through with their dues was amazing. I immediately fell in love with the process.

As far as what I was witnessing, everything was running as smooth as butter. I counted seven hoe-bitches between both cuddies. All bad bitches!

After each one of them dropped off their stack, they went back to the Ave to bust another date. That's when the vibe changed. There seemed to be a straggler pushing up to the Buick on Mac'n Louie's side. She was a sexy, short redbone in a cream colored skirt. Her hair curly and wet looking.

I say the vibe changed 'cause Lou got quiet when he saw her heading towards us. But by the way she was walking (hella slow), it didn't look like she really wanted to holla at him.

When she got to the car, she just stood outside Mac'n Lou's window not saying nothing. We all saw her, but no one addressed her, not even Lou. Instead, he turned towards

me and said, "Now, you've been seeing us clock dough ever since we got here, right?"

"Yeah," I said, knowing there was a method to his madness.

"That's one aspect of the game. It's how the 'ism is designed to play out. But sometimes you'll find yourself in a situation like this. See, young Dre, this pretty bitch fucked up. Look at 'er. She knows she fucked up."

All our windows were rolled down, so I knew she heard what he was saying. Yet, he hadn't actually said anything to her. And she hadn't spoken to him either.

"This triflin'-ass bitch been MIA all mothafuckin' day. She thinks this shit is play-play when it really ain't. Now, when I acknowledge this hoe, she better drop three to five stacks in my lap. If not, you're gonna get your first lesson in Gorilla Pimpin'!"

"Three to five?" I asked. "They making money like that?"

Pimpin' Te cut in, "Not in one day. Not on this blade."

"Hey, daddy," the cute redbone said.

I saw her drop something in Lou's lap. But it couldn't have been anywhere near the three to five stacks he expected because he quickly snapped, "What-da-fuck is this?!"

"It's six-fifty, daddy."

"You mean to tell me you been gone since this morning and this all you got? Bitch, you got me fucked up!"

"What'chu mean, daddy?"

Her reply obviously wasn't what the cuddy wanted to hear because Mac'n Lou immediately went mainy! Without any warning whatsoever, bruh snatched the door open and hopped out. She was just as surprised as I was. She looked terrified though.

Lou reached for her arm, but she snatched away hella quick. When she did that, he reached for the closest thing which was her top. He took ahold of her blouse and ripped it off. She had big-ass titties. I know this because they bounced out as soon as they were freed from confinement.

When her top came off she tried to cover herself but that was the wrong move. It gave Lou the chance to grab her. He took a handful of her hair and snatched her up. She started screaming. Cars were passing by seeing everything. Some slowed down but no one stopped to help her. Which was smart 'cause they would've gotten stomped out for getting involved in some shit that wasn't anyone else's business.

The cuddy didn't seem to give a fuck who was watching. He was hot? He slapped the taste out that girl's jaw. Then he hit her with a three piece and a biscuit. Cutie with the curly hair covered her head with her arms and balled up. That didn't help much. Lou just started booting that hoe like a soccer ball. When she fell onto her side he started stomping her out for real.

Blood was flying everywhere. I got out the car while he was kicking her and I saw her leaking. Her mouth, nose and head was oozing blood, he really fucked her up. After a while, she just laid there on the pavement knocked out.

There were people everywhere, yet no one even looked like they wanted to get involved. Mac'n Lou finished her off with one last boot to the chin. Then he spit on her before turning around and getting back in the Buick. I got back in too. Then we left.

"You saw that 'ism, Dre?" Mac'n Lou exclaimed as we drove away. "Sometimes you gotta get off in a bitch ass!"

Then Pimpin' Te cut in, "Pay attention, cuddy. This is all A-1 Gorilla Pimpin' at its finest."

Then, as Te maneuvered the extra large scraper into traffic he tossed a bag of weed in my lap. To Lou he said, "We gotta get you cleaned up. You got that hoe's blood all over your pants."

"Stop at the gas station across the street. I'll clean up in the restroom."

We pulled up to the 88th Street gas station across the street from where Lou had just left the broad laid out. They hopped out after telling me to roll up some trees with the papers that were in the glove compartment.

It took me a few minutes to roll up a couple dubees. When I finished I took the zags and the bag of weed and leaned over the front seat so I could toss it all back in the glove compartment. As I was doing that I heard a loud bang coming from behind me. It caught me off guard making me jump. That caused me to hit the yellow trunk release button in the glove compartment. And that's when all hell broke loose!

As soon as it happened I knew I had opened the trunk. I was about to hop out to close it when I felt some movement coming from the trunk. It made me look back and that's when I saw the trunk fly open. A second later, I heard some screaming coming from the back of the ride.

Right when that happened, Pimpin' Te and Mac'n Lou came running towards the whip from the far side of the gas station. Mac'n Louie ran towards the back of the Buick. When I realized what he was doing I followed suit. That's when I saw the girl who was screaming.

It was a white girl. She was asshole naked, running across the busy intersection yelling

for someone to save her.

Te had already hopped into the driver's seat. Louie doubled back quick. He shut the trunk and rushed to get back in the load. I was still standing there in shock when he yelled, "Get in, cuddy! We gotta get up outta here!"

CHAPTER TEN

"Execute stage 2, put the turkey in the oven..."
-Mac Dre

The door wasn't even shut when the scraper burnt rubber into traffic.

"We gotta get that bitch back in the trunk before the police see her!" Pimpin' Te bellowed. He hit the street sideways, fishtailing into traffic.

"Fuck!" Louie yelled.

When I saw the expression in his face, I followed his eyes and saw the naked white bitch running towards a green drop top Mustang.

"There he go right there!" Louie announced.

"Who?" I asked. "Who's she talking to?"

The runaway hoe-bitch was frantically explaining something to the driver of the Mustang. We were going in their direction, but the cuddy didn't stop. As soon as we passed 'em up the bitch started yelling something while wildly pointing in our direction.

"That's Leon," Louie explained. "He's her pimp."

"Damn!" Te said. "The nigga just busted a U! Pull out the heater, my nigga!"

The Mustang left the hoe-bitch in the middle of the street butt-ass-naked. When I looked back I saw him speeding towards us dangerously weaving in and out of traffic trying to catch up with us.

That's when I knew it was gonna get ugly. Lou came out the cuts with something extra large and chrome. It had to have been a .357.

Then, I heard several gunshots and the back window exploded. Shards of glass were all over me.

"Get down, cuddy!" Te yelled. "Lay down!"

"BOOM! BOOM! BOOM!" blasted Mac'n Lou's cannon. The cuddy was indiscriminately bustin' back from the interior of the Buick we were in.

BLADADAH! BLADADAH!

BOOM!BOOM!

BLADADAH! BLADADAH! BLADADAH!

I don't know what the nigga in the Mustang was bustin', but it was some heat!

Jay fishtailed into a few corners but he couldn't shake the sports car. That's when we started hearing sirens in the distance. The cops were out there. Leon must've heard them too because he aborted his mission, disappearing into traffic.

We were back on the freeway on our way to Vallejo a few minutes later. The cuddies were hot! I knew they blamed me for letting the hoe-bitch out the trunk, but if you asked me I didn't think it was all my fault. It's not like I knew she was back there.

Either way, it was apparent they were blaming me for the night's debacle. They were so mad they didn't even take me all the way home. They had to switch cars and rush back to the blade to pick up their other hoes so I ended up getting left at the front of the Crest and had to walk the rest of the way home.

Needless to say, my formal lessons on pimping were officially over. Still... watching all them females drop the bag in their laps ignited a flame that never left me. It was a lesson that taught me that bitches will pay a real nigga on general principle. From that day on, every bitch I ever came in contact with had to pay for my time.

The next day, me, Jay and Mall were at Coolio's house. We were hot boxing Jay's old green Maverick. I was telling them about the previous night's escapades and them niggaz thought it was the funniest story ever told.

"... What I wanna know is how the fuck did the bitch get in the trunk?" Jay teased.

"Fuck dat!" Coolio said. "How big were her tittles?"

"What about the booty?" Mall asked.

"Man, y'all trippin'!" I told them. "I almost got killed last night and all you can think of was titties and ass! Gi'me the mothafuckin' blunt!" I snatched the Vega from Mall. Then I got at Jay, "I told you already. It was an accident. When she kicked the back of the trunk, the car shifted and that shit knocked my hand into the release button."

I took a couple puffs then passed the trees to Da Unda Dogg. "To answer y'all questions about her cakes; Yeah, she was nice. Big tits and ass!"

"She probably ain't got no more teeth by the way you said Lou was beatin' her ass," Mall commented.

That lightened up the mood even more. Everybody started laughing. "He was stomping the fuck outta baby," I commented.

"On some real shit, I can be a pimp," Mall said. "I ain't got no problem selling a bitches BJ's, ass and pussy!"

"You probably can," I agreed. "You's a slick-talking pretty boy. The problem is we tryna get our bread right now. And you ain't got no hoe-bitches right now. We need some bread like right-right now."

We all got quiet for a minute. Everyone had to have been thinking how to make a mil' ticket over night.

Coolio was the first to shatter the silence, "What if we hit some licks? The cuddies hit a pawn shop a couple months back and them niggaz came up hard!"

"You right," I said. I thought about it for a minute and knew it was something worth looking into. The homey, Kimario and his bros hit some licks and they all had brand new cars. They wasn't much older than us, either.

As I scanned the cuddies faces, none of them looked as if they had a problem with the route the conversation was taking. So I asked them what they thought about it.

Jay looked out the windshield. He had the blunt in his hand. It was almost finished. After a few moments he turned to me in the passenger seat and said, "I'm wit' that type of shit, cuddy. We can do it."

Coolio was in the back seat behind him. He nodded like he was with it too, and said, "I ain't got no problems running up in some shit, cuddy."

That's when Mall said some shit that began a turf wide trend. "We can hit some pizza places, y'all. My relly's baby momma used to work at Mountain Mike's and she said they'd make three to four thousand a night on the weekends. She told me they had a safe too. One night we were at her house smoking and watching movies, she told me all kinds of shit. Like how the manager empties the safe and walks the cash to the bank a block away every Monday morning."

"Why Mondays?" Jay asked.

"I asked the same shit. She said Fridays, Saturdays and Sundays were their busiest days. But since Sundays are when the banks are closed, everything had to wait 'til Monday to get deposited."

Again, the smoky cabin of the '73 Maverick went silent. Everyone was digesting what they had just heard. In my head it all made sense. As a unit, we had never really robbed anything at gunpoint. But we all had experience laying shit down. We all had guns and ski masks. It seemed as if it was a natural transition for us.

"We can do this," Coolio said.

I agreed.

"We need to holla at Curt," Jay said. He started up the car and we got to moving. "If we gonna do this, we might as well go big!"

"Whatchu mean?" I asked.

"You know how we be hittin' house after house when we really be on one? Well, think about how much bread we can hit for if we went at them pizza parlors like that. We can hit Domino's, Straw Hat and Mountain Mike's all in one day…"

Just like that, me and the louies got on one. We went straight to Kilo Curt's house. When we got there, his little sister answered the door, scoffed at us and walked away leaving the door open.

Mall was quick with his comments, "What-da-fuck-wrong wit' you!?"

"Fuck you, Mall," she replied lightning fast.

Jay cut in just as fast, "Leave her alone, cuddy. Don't get that girl started."

"You better walk away, ugly-ass nigga," we all heard her mutter from the next room.

We found Curt in his room playing Nintendo. After shutting the door behind us, we laced 'im up on what we was contemplating. He was with the movement from the gate.

See, that's why I love my niggaz. Anytime one of us ever brought an issue to the table, we'd come together and brainstorm 'til we figured it out. It's like we all fed off the same energy. That's why we went on so many missions together.

Once Curt was on board, we didn't waste any time. We immediately pressed play. The plan was for us to hit three different pizza places. All after another. So we started stalking them.

Since they were spread out across the V, we had to split up in order to watch them. We rented dope fiend rentals for that. Then we'd switch up; one night, me and Mall would watch the Straw Hat on Sonoma Boulevard while Jay and Coolio sat on Mountain Mike's at the Gateway Plaza. The next day, Curt and Mall would watch the Dominos at the fairgrounds. Afterwards we'd exchange notes on what we saw.

Our missions brought us a gang of intel. Night shifts were way busier than day time. I remember Unda Dogg pushing for us to hit them on a Friday or Saturday night 'cause we'd get more loot. He figured since they would be filled with customers we'd be able to rob everyone eating there too. That idea got thrown out real quick. We all agreed because the risk was way too high.

We really gave these missions a lot of time and energy. It was like a job. We'd rent scrapers from smokers then go watch the spots we planned on hitting. We even came up with the best escape routes. All back streets. We chose routes that took us through residential areas instead of busy roads.

Guns weren't an issue. We had plenty of those from all the flocking we had been doing. On top of that, we could always count on Coolio when it came to weapons. He collected toasters. In the end, we came up with two shotguns, a big-ass .44 Magnum, and a German .22 with a clip and a screw off barrel.

We plotted for three weeks before pulling the string of robberies we schemed on. We decided on pulling the licks during the day time because there would be less traffic.

That also meant our getaway would have to take place in broad daylight. Which wasn't gonna be a problem since we were conscious of all the possible witnesses along the way.

Kilo Curt was the designated driver. He had handles. The cuddy also had sense, so we wouldn't have to worry about him speeding away from scenes when it wasn't called for.

We even discussed little details like when was the best time to slide the bandanas and ski masks over our faces before running up in the pizza places. No one wanted a good Samaritan to walk up and see some shit they didn't need to see.

The night before the licks were 'posed to go down, Mall got snatched up and taken to juvenile hall. The cuddy was on juvenile probation and kept skipping school so they took him in. That left us with me, Jay Diggs, Coolio and Curt. The discussion did come up about us bringing in another cuddy, but we decided against it 'cause there wasn't a need for it.

We had two stolos for the juxt. One for the work; the other for the getaway. The attire for the day was black everything. Jay and Curt took the sawed-off shotguns. Even though Curt was supposed to stay in the car the whole time he still had the shotty in case shit got ugly. I had the big-ass .357. That bitch was a cannon! Jay toted the other Street Sweeper and Coolio carried the German .22. We didn't plan on shooting anyone but we were more than willing; and definitely able to lay a mothafucka down if shit got that level.

Straw Hat was the first pizza place we pulled up on. Curt took the front door like he was being called out for a race. I ain't gonna lie. I was nervous as fuck! That didn't stop shit though. We were outlaws on a mission.

Things got loud the moment we blitzed. Me, Jay and Coolio barged in wearing ski masks and bandanas. Jay got a loud, deep voice, so he was the one yellin': "This a mothafuckin' robbery! Get with the program and there won't be no problems!"

There were customers in there. A couple females screamed at first, but Jay shut all that shit down immediately.

I hopped over the counter with an empty duffle bag strapped to my back and went straight for the manager. Coolio followed suit. He held the few employees in place while I took their boss to his office. My face was covered, yet that toaster was so close to his face that I doubt he would've recognized me if I was bare faced.

I had robbed a dice game or two before that day. Putting a pistol in a mark's face wasn't all that new to me. However, robbing a street nigga is different than running up in a legal establishment. A real block bleeder will always give a little resistance. Even if it's just in his eyes. The manager I had at gunpoint wasn't anything like that. He led me straight to his office with no resistance.

The Game Gods were definitely fucking with us at that point in time. We had came in at the prefect moment. The manager must've been counting his change a little while earlier 'cause there were stacks of cash on his desk. All the ones, fives, tens, twenties and fifties were neatly stacked with rubber bands already on them!

"Here! It's all there," he assured me. "Take it and go! Take it all..."

"Here!" I tossed him the duffle. "Fill it up!"

The whole time he was dropping the paper in the bag, I had that thang in his face. The barrel was so close to his nostrils, I'm sure he could smell the gunpowder. Once the duffle was filled I had him lay down on the floor. Then I made my exit.

The cuddies were waiting on me. The whole thang only took a few seconds. We were in and out in a flash. Curt had the load already in gear. As soon as we hopped in, he took off smooth, as if we had just picked up some pizza and were on our way back to the house.

We were juiced!

"We did that, cuddy!" Coolio celebrated.

"Bruh, check it out!" I said before I opened the duffle and showed the louies what we had.

"It's on!" they said. "We killin' the game!"

"A'ight, louies," Curt said. He was studying the rearview as he skillfully pushed through traffic. "Y'all gotta duck down. Tuck the cash and get ready for the next lick."

"You right," Jay agreed. "We gotta keep our head in the game, cuddies."

We simmered down but I know my niggaz were just as hyped up as I was. That juxt opened the gate for our inner beasts to come out. The evolution of our gang was taking place right then and there. A successful lick will do that to a crew. Pulling it off was too easy and extremely fast. Personally, I couldn't wait to hit the next one!

The next spot was a Domino's but it was only set up for deliveries. It was next to the fairgrounds. Since nothing big in the city was happening at the time, we figured our exit would be clean too.

Kilo pulled us up at the rear of the joint. As we circled around it, I noticed something about the Domino's that was different than Straw Hat's. Even though there were less customers there was a bigger crew of employees. After pulling up in the alley behind it, me and the cuddies got out and slithered towards the front entrance. Coolio was in front of me, so he was the first one of us to confront the two white boys who were posted up outside.

We walked up on them just as we were sliding our masks on. They caught us off guard, but instinct took over real quick. One of the guys looked like he was our age. The other was older, with a beer gut. Coolio took to this ski mask game like fish do to water. He didn't even blink. That pistol in his hand was in the younger boy's stomach before any of them knew what was happening. I immediately fell into sync with 'im. I put my thang in the older man's face.

"Let's take this party inside, fellas," Coolio ordered them.

"You heard 'im," Jay chimed in before they had the chance to think about what they had been told to do.

As soon as we entered the building the employees eyes all let us know they knew exactly what was happening. One bitch screamed, two others took off running towards the back of the kitchen.

"BOOM!"

Unda Dogg let off a shot. Pieces of the ceiling suddenly rained all over us.

One of the workers who did her ten yard dash stopped in her tracks. The other girl didn't, though. She made it out the back. In my head, all kinds of alarms went off.

Jay wasn't bullshitting. "Get the money!" he told me.

The guy I had my gun on pleaded with us, "Don't do anything crazy, guys "

"Shut-up!" I spat. "Where's the safe?"

His eyes cut towards an older Hispanic woman who was standing next to a group of three other employees. I saw the exchange and knew what it meant.

"Watch 'em," I told the cuddies. Then I trained my weapon on the Mexican lady. "You already know what it is. Take me to the safe before shit gets ugly!"

She did as she was told. She led me to the office. The safe was on top of the desk right there out in the open. She went straight to it and started fiddling with the knob.

I kept thinking about the mothafucka that made it out the back. I knew we were pressed for time. That added to the stress the shaky bitch was causing me. Her hands were trembling so much she kept having to start all over. For a second, I thought she was stalling for time, but when she started crying I knew she was just nervous.

"Check it out, auntie. You good. Ain't nobody gonna get hurt as long as you open that safe. Don't worry about shit. Go ahead and breathe. You a'ight, auntie. You good," I assured her.

It worked! She busted that bitch open real quick. I handed her the bag so she could add to the pot. As she started dropping the loot in the duffle I could see they didn't have as much money as the last one. It seemed like a cool amount, but it was less. Either way, it was gonna have to do.

"A'ight, auntie. Get on your stomach. "Give me a few minutes then you can get up."

"Okay-Okay," she replied nervously.

The second I stepped out the office I motioned for the cuddies to follow me. They had the rest of the Domino's crew laid out. We all ran for the back door. That's where Curt had the car waiting on us. I busted through the exit first. As soon as I hit the open air I was slapped with a scene I wasn't expecting to see.

Curt had the runaway Domino's employee face down on the pavement. He was standing over her with the shotty pointed at the bitches cranium...

CHAPTER ELEVEN

*"I'm gonna get as many digits that's on my license plate.
Then I'ma shit on these midgets. Bitch, I can't wait!"*
-Mac Dre

"**D**on't look up, bitch!" Curt growled. He motioned with his head for us to get in the ride, just as he stuffed the muzzle of his gauge into her head. Once we were all in, he got in too. With the peddle to the metal he swerved up outta there.

"What-da-fuck happened?" he asked angrily.

"She just took off, cuddy," Unda Dog replied. "I wasn't 'bout to shoot her in the back. But I-"

"I think the first two saw our faces," I said, recalling the moment we walked up on the first set of Domino's employees.

"What?" Curt asked. "What the fuck happened to y'all masks? That bitch I had on the ground definitely saw me too!"

"Man," Jay began.

"The cuddies hit the corner too fast. Two people saw them, but that shit was quick."

"Fuck all'at!" I said. "We good! All we gotta do is get this last lick out the way and we're done!"

"Yeah," Curt said. "But, this time, y'all need to have your mothafuckin' masks on from the gate. And, Coolio... try not to shoot anybody, cuddy. We coming for the money, not they souls."

"We gotta hurry and get to the plaza. That last bitch saw the car, y'all. We need to handle our business quick so we can ditch this bitch!"

We got to Mountain Mike's in record time. I'm sure we got there before the VPD got to the fairgrounds. Nevertheless, we all knew we were on short time. This had to be an in and out job. With the shot fired at the last spot, it was only a matter of time before the whole city was swarming with pigs.

It was all business the moment we pulled up to the plaza. Luckily, it wasn't crowded. But there were people shopping at several of the other shops. Still, no pedestrians were visible. That made the whole vibe feel straight. Mountain Mike's had a few people inside. Not enough to slow down our push, though. We were intent on making that lick happen. We ran up in that bitch like beasts!

Jay was on his tip! "Everybody get down now! Anybody move and all-a-y'all gettin' it!"

There were only two occupied tables and Jay laid them down on the spot. Coolio held the employees at bay like a champ. He corralled them all into the walk-in freezer like it was a county jail holding tank. This time, nobody ran! And the cash... The cash was major! I took the manager to the back and filled up the rest of the sac.

Curt was waiting for us in the back, behind the restaurant. Man, that juxt went down flawlessly. We hopped in the ride and slithered into the shadows like planned.

After that, we went straight to the waterfront where the getaway car was. We had decided not to make the last leg of the trip in the stolo. Instead, we hopped in Kilo's scraper and slid back to the Crest. We pulled up to Jay's momma's house less than twenty minutes later.

Back then we weren't using the term "hyphy." But, looking back on that day, as we dumped the money from the duffle bag's onto Jay's bed, the only way to describe the vibe was pure hyphy! Me and the louies were going bonkers! That was the most money we had all, each individually seen at one place at one time!

CHAPTER TWELVE

"My game gets sicka' when the game gets thickai!
- Mac Dre

We was really on after that. All that money had a nigga thinking on a whole different level! It was the most cheese a nigga had ever seen up to that point. Years later, I counted twenty and thirty times that much. But that night, we thought we was the richest niggaz in the Bay.

After counting it up it came out to just over forty G's. It was four of us. That put us all at ten racks a piece. Now, you gotta keep in mind that we were all still going to Hogan High. Flocking was our main hustle. It fed us for a while. But that was next level shit.

You know, as I think back on that night I could only think of one flaw. I don't think any of us really knew what to do with all that money. In a way, we weren't prepared for that shit. Me and the cuddies were real flossers, though. We did what any other group of young niggaz would've done.

Coolio copped 'im a whip real quick. Not only did he get a load, he also bought a gang of clothes and some shiny gold. You couldn't tell the louie shit when he hit the turf in his candy apple red Skylark on Daytons.

Jay did the same thing. He bought an old school Lac' though. He kept it on stock rims and invested in the beat. Four 18's was beating up his trunk every time he decided to stunt on the less fortunate.

Curt spent a lot of his bread on guns. He also got an apartment in Fairfield that no one knew he had. Kilo's my nigga, but real talk, I didn't even know where his honey comb hideout was. I wasn't even mad at him for it either.

All my niggaz went in with me and we rented the Hall at The Courtyard. It was a spot built by Marriot where you could throw parties. I'll get to that in a minute. But first I'ma put you up on what I did with my money.

I was still trippin' off how legit 40 and his niggaz tape covers looked like. They was on some professional shit and I was trying to beat them on every level. So I went on a mission. I bought some hip hop magazines and quickly started calling the companies who advertised in the back. There was a company that made album covers for a cool price. When I called them they told me to send them some pictures of myself and give them a theme to work with. It was exactly what I needed.

I definitely invested in my music career. That was a must. But that didn't mean I didn't hit the turf correct. There was a '64 Mustang I had seen parked on the side of a house next to the high school that I had my eyes on for a couple summers. As soon as I got on, I went to the house it was parked at and knocked on the door. I got that bitch for twenty-two hundred. After giving it a full tune up, some new rims and tires and some beat I was burning rubber all over the 'V.'

We was already 'dem niggaz at school when we'd pushed up there in Kilo Curt's whip. But after that lick we all had rides. Clean shit!

We was the only crew that age that was all high siding like that. I can't help but smile when I think back on those days 'cause we were the opposite of humble. We was on one and couldn't no one tell us shit!

You know... Hogan High helped me blow up. High school actually gave us a platform. See, nowadays social media is how you get the word out about what you doing. Back then it was different. Word of mouth made the world go around. I passed out hundreds of demo tapes and that's what got our initial buzz popping. On top of that, we was pushing so hard we couldn't help but attract attention to ourselves.

At the time, the Romper Room was about 15 deep. At first, we would rent dope fiend's cars or push stolos when it was time to mob. But now we had 4 cars and they were all clean. It was common for us to push everywhere at least 16 to 18 deep. This was how we moved every single day. We felt untouchable.

After I got the demo tape covers printed up I gave The Mac a few. I'll never forget the smile he gave me when I presented them to him. Cuddy was real player about it. He was sincerely happy for a nigga. He took 'em and promised to give a copy to different people who could help push my movement. That's not all he did either.

He also told me he was going to give a copy to his nigga at KMEL (the local radio station). That move right there was probably the most beneficial move made on my behalf up until that point.

The first year I passed my tapes around at school it gave me a rush. It gave me a sense of accomplishment. Made me feel like I was doing something. But this was different. After me and the louies hit those licks it put us on a whole different level. Now, we were on display for the whole city. It made us famous. It actually gave me the first glimpse of what the rap game was gonna do for me and my niggaz.

It really hit me after we did our first show. The Courtyard is a hall that holds about 600 people. It cost us $1500 to rent it for a night. When we first discussed renting the hall and doing a show, we all knew we were gonna be puttin' on for the whole city. It wasn't the first time we got on stage if you counted the talent shows at school. But it was bigger because it wasn't just gonna be people we went to school with. It was gonna be the first time we performed for people from other ghettos.

We went dumb on the flyer tip. After getting a thousand flyers printed up, we spent two weeks driving around the city passing them out. Hogan High's hallways were saturated with them. I'll never forget the time when the principal came to my homeroom one morning with an arm full of them talking 'bout I needed to stop putting them all over the school. That shit was hillarious!

Renting the hall and passing out flyers were just two steps that had to be taken. The next was hiring a DJ with all the equipment needed to broadcast a show in a hall that big. The Mac helped us with that. After that, we were ready!

At the peak of my career I was doing 5 to 6 shows a week to crowds 100 times that size. But, at that time in my life that show was the biggest event in my world. The anticipation of it all was out of this universe. We were all getting more and more excited the closer we got to the show. I ain't gonna lie, for a minute I felt myself getting a little nervous. Some people can't handle performing in front of large crowds. Even though I knew all the songs and had performed them in front of people before, I couldn't help but feel I might fumble when the curtain call came.

The night the show was to go on, the hall was packed. Bad bitches and reputable gangstaz were everywhere. They were loud as fuck too. Of course there were way more than 600 people in that mothafucka'. The crowd was thick! The pressure was on. But the moment the microphone hit my hand, I didn't think twice. I went all the way dumb!

That shit was as natural as if I was born with a mic in my hand. It was the same as if I was spittin' in a cipher with the cuddies. It was no different than when me and the louies would freestyle inside Kilo Curt's ride. That shit was fun!

That night showed the city that me and the cuddies were a problem. We tore that mothafucka' up! At times, the whole crowd rapped along to the lyrics we were spittin'. They already knew the words! That shit was exhilarating!

What a lot of people don't realize is that their biggest haters will come from their own hometown. Your city is the hardest field to conquer because a lot of people feel like it should be them on whatever stage you performing on. I've seen haters rip posters off walls, throw flyers away and stomp on niggaz demos as soon as the nigga walks away from handing it to them.

We didn't have to deal with that passive aggressive bullshit. Yeah, the opps were niggaz from 40's camp. But they were a nonfactor. Not only did the Crest support us but we had the bitches behind us. Something we all learned early was if the bitches fuck wit' you, the niggaz will follow.

The Country Club Crest bred true players, pimps and ganstaz. We got a way with words. We got ways of making women feel like a million bucks. This is because we know the truth. Every woman is worth her weight in gold based on the fact that they all hold a treasure chest between their legs. If you spit that fire in they ear they'll exalt you above the rest.

And that's what me and the cuddies did naturally. It came like that because the Crest was imbedded in our DNA.

I'll never forget the rush that performance gave me that night. Ever since then, I've been chasing that feeling. I was born to be on that stage.

CHAPTER THIRTEEN

"I put my lips to her tits and softly bit down on one."
- Mac Dre

We were treated like superstars that night. The females were on our dicks like they were made of gold. After the show we stayed behind to help the DJ pack his shit.

The crowd had slimmed down but there were still a group of bitches that stayed behind jocking the cuddies. The louies had their pick of the litter. I could've chosen any which one I wanted but my mind was more focused on that door money. Not only was that how we were gonna make our bread back, but that was also how the DJ was gonna get paid.

Everything had calmed down by the time we ended up at a table in the back of the hall counting and splitting up the funds. At one point, an older white lady walked up to us wearing a tight-ass Black dress. Her body was banging. That dressed hugged all her curves while squeezing the best areas perfectly. I had saw her approaching us from afar so when she walked up to me and started talking I wasn't really caught off guard.

Baby started the convo' by giving me props on the show. Then she asked me if I smoked weed. That shit made my ears perk since I'm a certified pothead. So my reply was "Damn right, I blow Why? You got some dank?"

"As a matter of fact, I do. I got some bomb from Humbolt County in my room. I was actually wondering if you'd like to come hang-out and smoke with me."

Jay was sitting there listening to the whole exchange. He spoke up and said, "Shiiit, Let's go-"

"This invitation doesn't extend to your crew, Dre," she said calmly.

Kilo and the DJ smirked at the diss she shot at Jay. A lesser man in Digg's position would've lashed out. The cuddy didn't trip though. He peeped the play and was a player about the situation.

"You heard the woman," he said. "Go on, cuddy. We got this. We'll catch up wit' you in the morning."

I glanced at her then back at the cuddies. I wasn't really trippin'. The thing was, I had never really fucked with a white girl before. I wasn't gonna let that stop me though, so I left with her.

We took the elevator up to her room. She let me know she had a view of the water so I was looking forward to that. Watching the waters of the Bay always calmed me down. It gave me a sense of peace. Especially from a view that's up in the sky.

Once we got up there I settled in on the couch in the living room. When she excused herself to freshen up I got up and looked out that big-ass window. I'm telling you, that night was unique. Part of it had to be the fact that I had just performed for the largest crowd of my freshman career. I felt like I was sitting on top of the world.

When she came back, baby wasn't wearing that black dress no more. She was in a robe. Her hair was up, too. She was bad as-fuck! And, let me clarify something real quick. Earlier, when I said she was an older white lady, you gotta remember I was still in high school at that time. She was in her twenties, but to me, at that point in time, it was classified as older.

Anyways, she handed ya' boy the greenery and had me roll it up. We didn't even get halfway through the smokery before she said some shit that surprised the fuck outta me.

"So, Dre. How big is your dick?"

I coughed, "What?!"

"I watched you grabbing your crotch all night long. So it's got me a little curious."

She caught me off guard, I ain't gonna lie. But a Country Club Crest nigga always got a response for a bitch.

"I got ten inches on hang, ma!"

"Hell no! How old are you? Sixteen, seventeen years old? No way!"

"Shiiit! I can show you betta' than I can tell ya'!"

Man, that white lady didn't play! She reached straight for my belt, undid it and let the beast come out. By the time she unzipped my jeans my dick hopped out ready to do some damage. She took it in her hand and couldn't even wrap her fingers round it. One thing I'll never forget is how soft her fingers felt. She started stroking that mothafucka' and had me curling my toes hella quick!

"This thing'll be a new record for me, Dre! I'm not even sure I can take it but I need you to do something for me."

"What's that?" I asked.

"I need you to somehow, some way put this thing in my ass."

"Damn, ma! I ain't never did no shit like that before. In the booty-"

She caught me in my tracks! In mid sentence, I had to shut da' fuck up 'cause baby put her lips around the head of my dick and went crazy! Her wet tongue started twirling and I started squirming. Her mouth-game was tremendous.

After suddenly popping my shit out of her mouth she looked up at me and said, "I guess I'll be your first, eh?"

Then she started bobbing her head in my lap again. She popped it out her mouth after five or six dives and continued, "I never had one this big. So we'll both be trying something new tonight."

Man, that shit had my mind going crazy! Then, right after putting that thought in my mental, she slipped out her robe and went back to sucking. She was butt-ass naked. I took a look at her round, white ass and my dick jerked. She caught the vibe and started bobbing on it even faster.

"On some real shit," I told her. "I don't know to many bitches that can take this whole dick. That shit be getting on my nerves sometimes. I can't stand when females be running from this pipe."

"Well I'm not one of them little girls you're used to messing with. I'm a grown-ass woman."

"What made you step to me?" I had to ask.

"I can tell by the way your friends treat you that you're somebody. And, if you're not somebody yet, you will be soon. Didn't you see how the crowd reacted to you tonight? You're special, Dre."

She stopped slurping on my meat just long enough to tell me that. Then she went back to it. The whole time she was speaking she never stopped stroking the pipe with her right hand. But once the exchange was over, she got right back to the job at hand. Baby attacked this dick like she had a point to prove. She dived in face first.

After a minute of slobbing on my shit, she managed to get half of it down her throat. I gotta keep it gutta wit' y'all; I couldn't believe she was swallowing all that dick! I'll never understand how bitches can take swipe in they throat like they do.

She gripped the base with both hands and went to town. That shit felt so good, I started moving my hips to meet her in the middle. She gagged a few times, but she never lost her composure. Baby was going dumb on the swipe!

Then, out of nowhere, right when it really started feeling bomb - the bitch stopped! She snatched that muthafucka out her mouth and said, "You need to fuck the shit outta me, Dre! I want you to go as deep and hard as you can. Don't hold back, Dre."

She still didn't miss a beat. After giving me those directions, baby went right back to her mission. She took this dick back in her mouth and twirled her tongue all over the head. Fuuuck! that shit felt good!

After diving on it a few more times she came up for air and said, "I'm not one of these little girls you used to. But, I ain't gonna lie, I never had a dick this big. I don't give a fuck, though." She actually held my dick in her hand to display it's length and girth. "I know I can take it. I know I can."

I could tell baby wanted me to kill dat cat. Not too many females could ever take this whole dick, so I always eased into any and every sexual scenario I entered. This time it was different. That snow bunny was driving me crazy with all that talk about beating them guts up.

I knew she was ready when she finally got up. She stood up and gave me a three hundred and sixty degree view of what she was working with. It was the first time I really saw her body and I was cool with it. She had some melons with gumdrop nipples.

Her pussy was all the way bald which wasn't the norm back then. But, I was definitely feeling it. Something about how wide her hips were made me feel like maybe she really could take the dick. It just looked right.

I was still seated on the couch when she climbed on top of me. The first thing I remember feeling was the smoothness of her bald pussy lips rubbing against the tip of this hammer. She reached below herself, grabbed my swipe just below the head and started rubbing it against her clit. Her pussy started dripping all over my shit like some baby oil! Then, without any sort of warning she slipped that pussy over my mushroom.

"God, dayum!" I grabbed her hips and pushed her down quick. I did it before she had a chance to stop me. Usually, I would've never made that move. But, baby was talking that shit so I had to go hard.

Her pussy was so wet I slipped in easy-as-fuck. I pushed myself into her until there was about three inches left. She squealed too! She squealed loud and dug her nails into my forearms. But it didn't phase her. She raised up then dropped right back down! She didn't go as low as I wanted her to but I didn't care. That pussy fit like a glove and it felt good as hell.

Every time she raised up, I'd pull her right back down. Her pussy gripped and squeezed my shit tight. I ain't gonna lie, she kept dropping lower every time she came down. Her titties kept me captivated when they started bouncing so I took my hands off her hips and relocated them to her tits. Before I knew it, I felt her clit rubbing against my pelvis! She had finally gotten my whole dick in her pussy.

That shit was mainy!

"Fuuuck, Dre! Pinch my nipples! Grab 'em, Dre! Bite them!"

I put my lips on her tits and softly bit down on one. Again, I surprised her by grabbing her waist and slamming my hips into hers. She gave out a loud cry of pain but she didn't flinch! I stretched that pussy out in a good way. Once she got jackhammered like that she couldn't be stopped.

Her face took a different shape after that. Baby got serious. She reached down and took ahold of my hips. That's when she went wild. She held onto me and started riding my dick like a champ! I rammed myself into her too! Before long, the sound of our bodies slamming into one another was all you heard.

"Don't fucking stop, Dre!" she moaned as her booty cheeks slapped into my thighs. "Go harder, Dre! Oh-my-God! I'm gonna cum!"

She was going hella fast by then. I could tell she was about to bust one. She was at the edge. But I had different plans. I wasn't gonna let her get off that easy. I pushed her off me hella fast. As fast as I could, I stood up, snatched my pants off and bent her over the couch.

I'ma tell y'all right now: She was lucky her pussy had my dick so wet 'cause I was all gas, no brakes!

I lined up my One-Eyed Willy with her brown eye, and with one hard thrust I buried a whole ten inches of hard dick in that bitches anal cavity! She yelped loud as fuck; lost her cool and tried to run but couldn't. I had vise grips on her hips. I held her still. Her ass cheeks were touching my stomach while the head of my dick was in hers.

She had a cool three seconds to come to terms with my actions before I kicked into second gear. "Ohhh, fuuck!" she screamed. But I didn't pay it no mind. She said she wanted me to go dumb so I gave her the business. I went long, hard and fast. Slamming this pipe into her cheeks. Then, the surprise of the decade came. SHE shifted us into 3rd gear! She started pushing that ass back at me. The sound of our bodies smacking was deafening! She took the dick like a porn star!

We went at it like this for a minute. Then out of nowhere, I felt her booty squeeze my dick like vice grips. If my swipe would've been average she probably would've popped me out. But I was so deep in her shit I wasn't 'bout to get pushed out. So I kept diggin'!

"I'm cumming, Dre! I'm cumming, mothafucka'!"

That made me really go stupid! I went even harder while gritting my teeth and gripping her cheeks. I killed that cat! In 4th gear, I hit her with short, quick thrusts! Pulling out maybe 3 inches before slamming back into her.

She was screaming by then. Her right hand reached behind her and pushed on my hip so I couldn't go all the way in. That shit turned me on even more 'cause it let me know she was on the verge of tapping out. Damn, that night was raw!

In the end, I blew a thick-ass load in her ass!

CHAPTER FOURTEEN

"The goal had always been to get rich off this music."
- Mac Dre

What I didn't realize at the time was my life was about to change in ways I could never imagine. I was at a major turning point in my career.

Something I've learned about the industry is persistence pays off. Even if you come from dirty soil, you'll eventually sprout. All you gotta do is work hard. Stay grounded and focus on the mission at hand. If your grind is solid you'll reach Jack and the beanstalk status.

I didn't know it at the time, but The Mac was watching the show we put on. I actually thought brody was out of town 'cause I hadn't seen 'im in a minute. He was in the building though. After leaving the white girl that next morning I ran into Mike-Mike in the lobby.

Brody had two white bitches carrying his bags. Them juicy-booty snow bunnies is what initially caught my eye. But when I saw the cuddy I lit up. The Mac in me wanted to act cool, but the cuddy in me stayed hyphy. I went straight up to him and said, "Cuddy! What's cracka-lackin'?!"

He met me with the same energy. "You! You's what's crackin'! I saw your performance last night, my nigga! You did your shit! You killed it, brody!"

We both headed outside into the early morning sun. The females paid our discussion no mind whatsoever. They just kept strolling.

"You should'a said something! We could've rocked the stage together! All the cuddies know your music. That shit would'a went crazy!"

"Naw, cuddy. That was your night to shine. You and the cuddies shined like stars last night. There's nothing on earth that could've made last night better. Plus, I'm not sure if you heard, but The Mac don't rap for free. And I hope you don't either. You got your dough for that show, right? The doorman was sure collectin' them ducats."

I smiled 'cause the cuddy was always serious when it came to that mulah. I had to stunt then. I reached into my pocket and pulled out my billfold. "Yeah, Cuddy. I got mines. A few of us put our bread together to throw the show. So we split the dough from the door.

We was headed across the parking lot as we continued to talk. "A'ight, check it. Don't go out and spend that money, bruh. Holla at the louies and get 'em to flip it on another show. Holla at some club owners. Rent another hall. Go to Richmond, Oakland, Pittsburg and Concord. Don't stop, Cuddy! Listen; your demo tapes are straight fire! I watched the crowd, cuddy. The crowd knew y'all music word for word! Most of 'em was from the turf. All of them were from the V. That's cool, but you gotta spread your fire like a wild fire if you really wanna blow. You gotta reinvest! Throw more shows! Don't quit while you ahead. You smell what I'm saying?"

"Yeah. I hear you, cuddy. That's what I'ma do."

By the time we reached his 'Lac his hoes were already inside. The car was running and it was pulling out the parking spot with a bad bitch behind the wheel. The last thing the cuddy said before getting in and riding away was, "Dre, you 'bout to blow up. Keep doing what you doing. Just don't stop. Don't slow down. Bite down and never let go!"

My mouth agreed with him. And my hand gave the louie dap. But it wasn't 'til I got behind the wheel of my whip that it really hit me. As I drove back to the Crest it registered into my mental. We had just did a show that made a profit. It was a hustle. So, just like any other grind, all we had to do was keep doing it. Stack up what we made and keep flipping it."

Music was our crack. The stage was our dope spot! The flame was officially lit.

The fire caught on and made itself apparent a few days later. Me, Coolio and Kilo Curt were on my momma's porch one afternoon just shooting the shit. We were still talking about the show we did and the bitches we fucked afterwards. Our cars were lined up back to back on the curb, giving us that rich clique look. We was some real wild young niggaz getting new money. Anybody with some eyes could see that.

I was just about to light up a blunt when my momma came out talking 'bout, "Dre, somebody from KMEL is on the phone wanting to talk to you."

Everybody's mouth dropped. I looked at her like she was crazy. What would the radio station want with me? It must've took me a minute to reply 'cause she got louder when she said, "Boy! I'm serious! The radio station on the phone! Come see what they want!"

We all got up and went inside. When I got to the kitchen I picked up the phone and heard, "Is this Mac Dre?"

"Yeah. This Dre. What up?"

"This is Chuey from 106.1 KMEL. Dre, I just got this tape from The Mac and I wanna play one of your songs on the air. Oh-and-I forgot to tell you; you're live on the air. Go ahead and tell our listeners who you are and where you from."

The moment he told me we were on the air I got on my hyphy tip for real!

"What's crackin', y'all! This Mac Drizzay coming from that Country Club Crest!"

"Dre, tell the Bay what you been up to. Let us know what you're about. The Mac been telling me about you. That you're the next biggest act to come out -"

"Ain't no actin' 'bout this Mac'n, Chuey! The Romper Room's the realest set to come out the V. We just finished doing a show at the Courtyard. We finna do another one this weekend. If you like what you just saw, come see us at the fairgrounds this weekend. And, if you didn't already see us in action you betta' hurry up before you get left behind."

"Y'all heard it here first. KMEL is always first to bring you the freshest music out the Bay Area -"

"Yee! Yee!"

"This is Mac Dre's new track called, *Too Hard For The Radio!*

When I heard him 'bout to play my song I covered up the mouthpiece and told Jay to hurry up and grab the radio. Then Chuey came back on the line.

"That was great, Dre!"

"Thanks, man!"

"Look, your music is raw! I'm gonna support you. Just keep it coming and I'll keep your tracks in rotation."

"I got'chu, Chuey! For real, I appreciate the backup!"

I hung up the phone just as Jay came in the kitchen with the boom box blasting my song! The goal had always been to get rich off the music shit. The thing was, before that day I can honestly say it was like a distant dream. But, hearing my voice on the radio finally made it real. The look in my momma's eyes gave me a dose of triumph too. She grabbed me and hugged the fuck outta me. My niggaz went dumb too!

Hearing my song on the radio that day convinced me that I was gonna make it with the music. Now, don't forget, we were all still in school. That next day was like walking the red carpet. We was already the flyest niggaz at Hogan, but that show put us over the top. Even the teachers had to respect it. Bitches that tried to fight the vibe before couldn't deny it no more. Now, they were on some aggressive shit, trying to catch up with the tables that were turning.

Personally, it felt like people were stepping to me like I was the most famous rapper in the world. And, you know what.. I was! Couldn't nobody tell me different. We was on some gangsta shit. There was a wave of energy I was riding and it was getting bigger by the minute!

There really wasn't a show at the fairgrounds that weekend. It didn't matter though. Chuey hit me up and said people had started calling the radio station nonstop trying to find out what happened. A rumor started that V.P.D. put a stop to it. Which was cool 'cause that just made mothafuckaz wanna see us even more. We ended up doing a skating ring in Fairfield two weeks later. Then a pool hall in Richmond. We went hard in them first few months. Hitting up all the local spots nonstop. That's what really cemented our support in the Bay.

When the Mac had that pep talk with me the morning after we did that show at the Courtyard I really took his words to heart. I understood the language he was speaking. There really wasn't a chance or a need to let the cuddy know how me and the louies came up with the money to throw that show. But it was on my mind. See, I learned years earlier that money makes money. The more money you have to invest means more money will come in.

At one point the conversation came up with the cuddies about some extracurricular shit. It was me, Kilo, Mall and Jay. We was all out in front of King's Market just posted up in front of Digg's ride. We was brainstorming on our next move and I just came out of nowhere with some mathematics...

"... So we already know that five bills will get us some cool tape covers, but no fliers. We can flip-"

"Yeah," Kilo cut in. "But, it was that show money that was fo' sho' money!"

Everyone laughed in agreement. The door money from the Courtyard show had brought us the most profit in the least amount of time.

That's when Diggs started stating what we had all been thinking. "If we ever plan on going big like them Hillside niggaz we can't think small. We gotta somehow print tape covers, rent studio time, do fliers and rent hall after hall and do show after show."

Curt replied, "On the Crest, I feel you, cuddy. I don't know 'bout y'all, but I got $800 in my pocket. Even if we all put our bread on the table it still won't be enough to do all that."

"Shiiit," Mall said. "What about them licks y'all pulled? It worked for y'all that first time. What about going dumb with it and get up all the money we need to do all that shit at once."

I don't know how it ended up the way it was, but the cuddies turned towards me. The conversation of licks came up and it was almost as if the decision was on me. There was one of two choices to be made. We could take it slow and grind it out. Or, we could take the ski mask route and turn that wave into a Tsunami.

At the time, the decision seemed like it was life or death. The risk was high, but then again, so was the profit.

In retrospect, I only took about thirty seconds to think it out. It might have seemed a lot longer than that at the time though. Regardless, the outcome was summed up in the words that left my mouth: "Let's mask up!"

CHAPTER FIFTEEN

"The bottom line is once we started robbing, everyone else did too."
- Mac Dre

Before we move on, I think it's important that I describe the temperature of the hood at that time. See... The Crest was a big neighborhood, but not big enough for people who live their not to know one another. Even though my immediate circle consisted of Curt, Jay, Mall and Coolio our crew was a lot bigger than that. The Romper Room was anywhere from 15 to 20 deep in them Crestside streets.

The whole clique was 100% active when it came to extracurricular movements that stemmed from the many 'ism's we were laced with. Some of the cuddies specialized in selling rocks, others flocked. We were all gangsta's about our paper though. The reason I'm taking these long strokes to paint this picture is so you can recognize the main factor in everything that ended up playing out.

Even though I'm putting you in the passenger seat of the rides I was in. These weren't the only rides taking place at the time. There were always at least three to four other crews the same size as ours that were pushing just as hard as we were. We might have been the only Crest niggaz making music at the time, but we weren't the only louies thuggin' the way we were thuggin'.

Let me take you back a few chapters to when I told you about that dice game in my momma's garage. You gotta understand how active my neighborhood was. It was an active ghetto. Each and every single member of the Romper Room was liable to have experienced a scene

exactly like that one in their own home at one point or another throughout their lives. In many ways, our lives were a shared experience.

When we hit them licks, word got around about what we did. Not only did we get away with it and shined; but we started doing it again and again. Next thing we knew, the rest of the Romper Room started doing the same shit. It got to the point where all of us were pulling licks. It wasn't just our generation who was doing it. Even the OG's got in on the gold rush. And what made matters even worse was there was a coke drought that year. This made a lot of niggaz who usually got their money peacefully to get off they ass and start putting pistols in people's personal space.

I'm assuming you know what a drought is. If not, let me explain: A drought is when for whatever reason, the cocaine supply goes dry. It gets real hard to find. If you do happen to locate a line on it the price will be extremely high. In the 1980's and 90's our stimulus packages came in the form of beige rocks. Because of that, most of the money that circulated throughout the ghetto had blood on it. Still, drug money paid rent, electricity, water and phone bills back then. Even if you weren't a dealer you still benefited from the drug trade in some way.

Since every day comes with a night you can't have good without bad. Since the economy was stimulated as the blood money flowed through its veins it was also crushed when the lines of communication with South America were blurred. A drought in the coke industry was the equivalent of a major industry like an oil refinery or car manufacturing plant closing down. Niggaz who were the bread winners in their family suddenly found themselves out of work. That created an atmosphere where dangerous career criminals became cold and hungry.

I think 40 Water once said, "The drought season is like Thanksgiving without the feasting."

That's gotta be one of the realest lines he ever wrote. The bottom line is when we started robbing, everyone else did too. No one was safe. Every single business establishment in the city became a target. Ice Cream trucks, laundry mats, pizza parlors, grocery stores, even hotels and motels were game. What made the game even colder is that we weren't really getting caught. The cuddies would take their time plotting on licks as if they were military movements.

We had a system that became more sophisticated with every robbery. Pizza parlors were the main targets. The cuddies loved them because they brought in the most money. But that soon led to us hitting banks. It was almost as if the pizza places were training us for the federal heists.

The first bank we hit was in Central Vallejo. I'm not gonna go into the name and date when it happened. But I'll describe it.

The lobby had two exits. One on each side. The whole building had large tinted windows on each side. Anyone inside could see outside, but passerby's couldn't really see inside. There were three tellers and a vault, but that doesn't mean it was a large bank. It really wasn't too much bigger than the average pizza restaurant.

The louies and I sat on that bitch for two weeks before we ran up in it. When I say we sat on it, I'm so serious. No exaggeration. We took 3 hour shifts watching that bitch six days a week from open to close. We knew the whole get down like clock-work.

Every morning at 7:30 a.m. the bank manager would come in. It was a middle aged white man with a bald head, clean shaven face and some glasses. He'd go in, do whatever he did, then by 8 the tellers would show up. There were only about 4 employees all together.

Once we figured out their schedule we concentrated on the next phaze of the operation which was the traffic surrounding the bank. Not necessarily the traffic of cars and pedestrians in the area. That was important too, but that's not what I'm talking about. I'm talking 'bout the business rush that comes in and out the bank at different times of day.

We quickly figured out banks had different rush hours than pizza places. Banks are busiest in the morning hours. They tend to slow down after nine a.m. Then they pick up between twelve and one. At four all the way until closing is a rush of business too.

The most pedestrian traffic comes in on Fridays. That's when most people got paid and wanted to cash their checks. We figured all this out real quick. So, after weighing out the pros and cons, our risk assessment brought us to the conclusion that the safest time to hit one was Monday through Thursday between ten and eleven a.m. Anytime sooner or later brought us the risk of running into too much foot traffic.

It was Diggs who made a connection between pizza parlors and banks that changed the game for us. We already knew Sundays were the most profitable days for us to hit a pizza place 'cause most of them kept their weekend earnings on hand until Monday morning.

Well, one day when I was in the car watching a bank with Diggs he said some shit that made a lot of sense. He pointed out that since pizza parlors deposited their bread on Mondays then maybe all the other local businesses did the same thing. Which meant Mondays were when banks were the chubbiest. It made sense to me.

We had all the employee schedules down. The best day to hit was figured out. Next was tailoring the safest getaway route.

That part was easy. Just like all the other licks we did, we'd definitely show up and show out in stolos. After pulling the juxt we'd drive a few miles to where our own cars would be parked. Hop out; hop in; split up; and meet up later to count and split the bread.

The first heist went smooth as butter! Since Mall had been tripping off not being in on the first few robberies we most definitely brought little bruh along for the ride. Plus, both, Coolio and Mall knew how to steal cars hella good. They stayed fucking with a Filipino clique called TNP so we kept stolos parked in alleys and abandoned garages. On the Saturday before the first bank lick was lined up, Mall showed up at my momma's house in a PG&E van. I ain't gonna lie, that move surprised the fuck outta me!

A few of us were posted up on the porch when he pulled up. As soon as he hopped out and made it around the front of the van I was like, "What-da-fuck!"

Mall jogged up to the porch beaming from ear to ear. He must've seen the surprise on our faces 'cause his first words were: "What's wrong?"

"Cuddy!" I said, damn near speechless. "Where the fuck you get that van?"

"From the PG&E parking lot," he replied. "We can use it for the lick!"

"What-da-fuck!" Kilo commented. "It says PG&E across the side of it. It's hella big, cuddy! And what the fuck we 'posed to do with that ladder?"

Me and Diggs busted out laughing.

Coolio's jaw was wide open.

Curt started clowning. He walked up to the van yelling, "What-da-fuck we 'posed to do with this, cuddy?"

Mall's smile never wavered. It was as if he knew something we didn't. He just calmly went to the side of the van and slid the door open. Then he reached inside, took out an orange vest and held it up for us to see.

"Check this out," he said. "There's hard hats and face masks. We can wear all this shit and mothafuckas gonna think we work for the electric company. We won't even have to wear ski masks."

Coolio and Curt went up to Mall and looked at what he was talking about. Curt grabbed a vest, Unda Dogg picked up a hard hat and mask. After a few seconds they looked at each other. Then they turned towards me and Diggs and said, "It's on!"

The only thing left was to do it! That Monday came and we pulled up to the bank at exactly 9:48 a.m. Jay stayed at the wheel, calmly driving us right up to the East entrance of the bank.

Anyone who saw me, Kilo, Mall and Coolio step out the van in our PG&E uniforms wouldn't have given either one of us a second glance. All of us were strapped, but none of our sticks were visible. I'm telling you, the smoke screen was proper. We went up in that bitch like it was a Halloween party.

I didn't see no surprises when I stepped in the lobby. Three tellers and a manager. One of the tellers was dealing with a customer. The other two were off to the side talking. The manager was parked at his desk in his office off to the side. The whole place was a glass house, making everything they did visible.

Kilo was our spokes person on this one. Everyone was at attention when he yelled, "It's a mothafucking robbery! Anybody move and all of y'all getting shot!"

By then we all had our guns out. Coolio went into the manager's office and put his toaster to his head. Me and Mall hopped over the counter.

"Where's the deposits?" I holla'd at the terrified bank tellers. I had an army duffle bag out from underneath my fluorescent PG&E vest in record time.

The teller I was looking at when I yelled was a white girl who looked like she was in her early twenties. She was all business. She immediately pointed towards the far wall where I saw six bank bags on the top of a desk. They were the same bags armored truck drivers carried from location to location.

It was payday in my eyes. I rushed towards the bags. Stuffed three of them in my duffle then tossed it to Mall.

"Go, cuddy! I got the rest!" I yelled.

I grabbed two more bank bags and threw them over the counter to Kilo. He alley-ooped the first one to Coolio who was running out the office. Then caught the second one and went towards the exit with it. I took the third one and did the ten yard dash towards the door.

In the back of the van we went dumb!

"We rich! We rich!"

I know Diggs had to contain himself as he calmly carried us to safety 'cause the energy we were emitting was contagious!

A few minutes later, we pulled up next to Curt's bucket and transferred vehicles. The plan was to go to Curt's house to count the bread. By then all of us had had gotten quiet. I guess it was really starting to sink in that we had gotten away.

No one had to tell me we hit the jackpot 'cause I already knew it. The bags I grabbed were all extra-hella heavy. But that didn't prepare me or any of the Cuddies for what we saw when we emptied those bags on Kilo's bed!

Stacks on stacks on stacks!

In the end, we counted over a hundred racks! Me and the louies were turnt' up passed the max. While we were celebrating no one noticed Curt leave the room even though I could've swore I heard a phone ring in another room.

A few minutes into the celebration, as we were all throwing money in the air and Mall was making snow angels on the bed with the bread, Curt came in with a whole different vibe.

"Dre! Diggs! Cuddies!" Curt bellowed over the noise we were making.

"What?!" we asked.

"Somebody shot Mike-Mike! The Mac is dead!"

CHAPTER SIXTEEN

"The nigga who did it doesn't deserve a mention."
- Mac Dre

The Crest lost its mind when The Mac was killed. Michael was a ghetto superstar. A once in a lifetime type of nigga. Cuddy wasn't a rapper with a Pimp persona. He was the real deal. His resume was authentic. In real life he was a bonafied pimp who happened to rap. The fact that his lyrics were raw just added to his glow.

Let me explain something real deep to you. There's a lot of rappers out there who really can't rap. Some of them cats are the same ones your homies be trying to emulate. All they are is actors with skillful deliveries. Big labels with state of the art studios and raw producers can put enough glitz and glamour behind almost anyone to make them seem authentic. That's why there are so many one-hit-wonders who shine for the summer then disappear, never to be heard of again.

Every once in a while a real superstar will show up and the streets will make him famous. In order for this to happen the artist has to have two things: A skill. He's gotta be a true lyricist. And, the nigga has to be a real gangsta. If you don't know the true definition of a gangsta, you better not be in the game.

Michael Robinson aka The Mac was my nigga! He was really on his pimp shit. The Louie came up in the trenches just like the rest of us. That's why everyone loved him. I hate that he lost his life so early on. Especially since his career was barely in its infancy.

Any authentic Country Club Crest representa' can tell you the details of what happened to The Mac. The story's been told a million times.

The cuddy was in the hood, at Borge's Park. He was up there choppin' game with a few of his hoe-bitches. He had just bought himself a Mustang with the brains blown out. He had put gold Daytons on it and was killing the game with it. That day he was out there on his super fly tip.

The nigga who killed the homey doesn't deserve a mention. His name will forever be forgotten. He's a nobody. The murder was a mistaken identity case. The sucka had gotten robbed by another cuddy a few days before so he came through on some retaliation type shit.

Two of Michael's females had walked off for a moment. They went to the park's public bathroom to do whatever it was that they needed to do. Then, just as they were heading back to the 'Stang they saw the bum-ass-nigga creeping up on the Mac. Without any hesitation they immediately started bustin' at him the moment they realized something wasn't kosure. But in the confusion they caused, the gunner hastily killed the homey without getting a proper ID.

Michael's Mustang was a chameleon purple. Which meant in a certain light it looked black. That's what ultimately got him killed that day. The fact that his Mustang looked black when it really wasn't even that color.

Some people tried to blame the bitches that busted at the fuck-nigga. That didn't make no sense to me. I salute them broads with all the admiration and respect due to a real Street Marine. Even though their aim was garbage, their intentions were platinum.

One day, way before that afternoon The Mac laced me with some real wisdom. He told me a bitch was the reflection of her man. He constantly said females will only have as much game as the nigga who laces them. I think of that whenever I see the look of amazement on the face of a person who hears that story for the first time. Some people are surprised to hear about some hoe-bitches swinging hammers in their pimp's defense. But not me. Not at all. Not when it had something to do with The Mac. His hoes were trained by an upper echelon nigga.

The Mac was a year and three days younger than me. Yet, when it came to pimping his knowledge and expertise was elevated way beyond his years. He was bred to be a Mac!

That incident taught me the importance of lacing a bitch the right way. They knew exactly how to handle themselves in that situation. Instead of calling the police they called Kyree. That gave us time to do our research on his killer.

I shouldn't have to state the obvious. But for those of you who don't know how the street codes go: We went dumb on that nigga and his whole family. People were kidnapped, tortured and murdered. By the time we got to him his whole family hated him. We made them cry up a storm before his soul left this earth. And, strictly for the record; if I had a chance to do my part over... I wouldn't change a thing!

Meanwhile, I kept grinding. I put my all into the music. I took every cent I made and invested in studio time. Kyree produced my tracks, bringing them to the level they needed to be. Then he extended his hand even further. He dug into his black book of connects and changed my life forever.

I was in the studio when he got the call saying Ice Cube wanted me to go on tour with him. At the time, Cube was doing a West Coast tour. He was doing concerts from Los Angeles to Seattle. I was called in to open for him. That opportunity changed the game for me because it put me in front of people who hadn't even heard of me before.

Still, I couldn't let the streets go. During the weekdays I'd be huggin' the block with the louies. On the weekends I was rocking stages up and down the coast.

That's around the time the drought let up. Coke was back in abundance. You would assume things would have went back to normal. But they didn't. As far as the Crest was concerned a new norm had been created.

A lot of the louies never went back to selling dope. Niggaz had mastered the ski mask ways. If you were part of our clique you robbed shit. As simple as that.

The law lets a lot go when it doesn't affect the lighter side of the tracks. I'm sure we would've attracted less attention if we would've been robbing gambling houses or D-Boys. But that wasn't the case. We were young Black males from the ghetto robbing law abiding citizens whose skin tone lacked melanin. There was no way in hell they'd let that go.

The Crest was hot. McGraw was promoted to Sargent. He really didn't have to patrol the hood no more. But he did. Except now he was in unmarked vehicles. Not only did he use the turf as his new office he also assigned a whole task force to stop the robberies.

I remember right after I bought my first Beemer me and the louies were parked at King's Market shining like stars. None of us were committing felonies, but then again our whole lifestyle was felonious so it didn't really matter.

McGraw was parked across the street, in the shade, just watching us. I'm telling you, McGraw spent just as much time in the Crest as any of us did. We weren't doing shit and neither was he. Coolio was on some other shit, though. I think he was mad 'cause he wanted to light up a blunt but couldn't cause it would've given McGraw a justifiable reason to come fuck with us.

"You see that honky, Dre?" he said while he was muggin' the unmarked car. Da Unda Dogg had a toothpick in his mouth, switching it from side to side in an agitated manner.

"Fuck 'im, cuddy. Don't pay that bitch no mind, homey."

What Coolio did next was actually kinda funny even though it ended up starting some shit. He went straight to his ride, put in one of our mixtapes and turnt' that mothafucka up as loud as the speakers would take it. The funny part was the song he chose to play: *PUNK POLICE*!

At the time, *Punk Police* was one of the hottest songs I had out. But McGraw wasn't in agreement with us on that note. The honky got exactly what he wanted... A reason to come fuck with us!

He pulled into the parking lot and slammed on his brakes right behind our cars! It wasn't like we was about to flee, but we couldn't have driven off even if we wanted to. Anyways, after making a big scene out of blocking us in, he got out of his car with his partner following in his puny footsteps.

"Hey, Mac Dre. How you doing, little buddy," McGraw said hella sarcastically. "You guys mind turning this bullshit down?"

I didn't say shit. Coolio spit on the ground.

McGraw's partner grew some nuts and told Coolio, "Get against the car!"

"For what?" Coolio asked.

I saw it in the cuddy's eyes. He had that familiar look that I had seen hundreds of times. McGraw's lackey was about to get knocked out.

McGraw approached me while his partner went towards the cuddy. I looked at Coolio and slightly shook my head. All I kept thinking was, *Don't sleep 'im, cuddy...*

He seemed to have caught and understood my silent message and assumed the position. Next thing I knew, we were both in cuffs!

"What-da-fuck is this?" I demanded to know.

A few of the cuddies who were in the store and saw the commotion came out talking shit. It was about to get mainy for them pigs until the next the thing happened.

Suddenly, the whole block was bombarded by po-pos! City police and sheriff cars came in deep from all directions. A ghetto bird swooped in. Plainclothes cops came from all over the place and closed in on the parking lot. It was a set up!

"Got your punk-ass this time, Dre! This is a probation sweep!" sneered McGraw. "We're about to tear the Crest a whole new asshole, cuddy!"

"Man! I didn't do shit!" I yelled as they forced me and Coolio into the back of the cop car.

"Pop their fucking trunks!" McGraw barked. I'm sure we'll find some weapons. If not, we'll get something out of their houses!"

We sat in the back of that stank-ass cop car for two hours! It was fucked up, 'cause McGraw was right. They didn't find shit in the Beemer. But they got a strap out of Coolio's car. That punk-ass bitch charged me with driving without a license, though.

They swept the Crest that afternoon, taking 40 of us in on different cases and probation violations. I ended up spending the night in the County jail that night. It was some real bullshit!

The turf lost a few cuddies that day. They hit us with some robbery charges. Luckily most of the louies who caught felonies went to juvenile hall. Nevertheless, they were still gone for a minute which was fucked up.

It seemed like everything was coming apart for a minute. The Mac was killed. McGraw was on us. Cuddies were getting locked up back to back. Still, the Romper Room remained active.

Since the hood was hot, a few of us took the show on the road.

Don't forget, I was actually on tour when all of this was going down. I'd be gone from Thursday to Sunday nights following the West Coast tour with Cube. Ya' boy wasn't alone either. Me, Kilo, Diggs, Da Unda Dogg and Mall had hit the road. Looking back, I realize that once we went OT we really started balling. The playing field was bigger, allowing us to spread our wings in a real way...

CHAPTER SEVENTEEN

"Once you put some heavy metal in someone's face and see how easy it is to take their shit, a candle's lit. A candle that burns at both ends real quick."
-Mac Dre

It was the hottest winter ever! The law was everywhere. You couldn't go nowhere without getting harassed by the pigs. McGraw never slept. That bitch-ass honky had the Gestapo kicking in doors like they was jack boys!

The whole city knew what it was. The Romper Room was on one. It was damn near like a war. Except, instead of shooting shit, we was robbing shit. They'd arrest a cuddy and we'd retaliate by robbing some more shit.

We couldn't go back to the dope game even if we wanted to. The city was flooded, it was smothered in cream. In the Crest we couldn't eat like that though. You couldn't bleed the block while cops were steady patrolling the block the way they were. Not only did they arrest us for being Black, they made it to where the fiends couldn't even come through the turf to get some work. They were pulling over every car they didn't recognize. Everybody in the city knew it, too. So it kept a lot of people from coming to the turf for their illicit party favors.

In order for me to properly paint this picture I need to help you understand how deep of a crime wave was created. At the time, the Romper Room consisted of about fourteen or fifteen cuddies. All of us were hella-hella tight and had trained for the shit we was doing. Well, even though we were tight, we still had circles within circles. The cuddies who benefited from our training took that blueprint and shared it with their own circle of cuddies. Then they'd hit their own licks with their extended crew of cuddies. That's why our neighborhood was so hot.

The fact that Michael was gone affected our mentalities as well. I remember the night the cuddies took The Mac's killer's car and doused that bitch with gas at Borge's Park. Watching that bucket go up in flames represented a change in course for us all.

It's extremely hard to explain the vibe The Mac brought to the atmosphere we were all a part of at the time. He gave the whole 'hood a feeling of hope. As long as he was ducking in and out the Crest showing us there was another world out there for us we all knew we could do bigger and better things with our lives. He showed us we could make it out the ghetto without getting our hands dirty.

The fact is, me and the louies picked up the torch. We dived into the music game like it was sweet. The thing was, none of us were role models. We was one hundred percent dirt gang. We took what we wanted then flaunted it for the world to see. We were beasts!

That ski mask life was addictive. Once you put some heavy metal in someone's face and see how easy it is to take their shit, a candle's lit. A candle that burns at both ends real quick. When you got a team who's into the same movement, shit explodes.

It's like this: If you're at your homey's spot smoking and chillin', and someone says, "Y'all wanna hit a bank?" Two things can happen.

1. Ya' cuddies can laugh it off. Tell you you're trippin'. If that happens, the idea gets no life. It dies.

2. One of your dogs can say, "Shiiit, I'm wit' it." Now it's two of y'all on the same hype. That energy alone is enough to turn the rest of your cipher into gun-wielding psychos.

Imagine being in a house with 14 or 15 hungry niggaz. Niggaz whose willing to do whatever to eat some steak with their beans and rice. Especially when there's a way to get it easily. When you're in an environment like that, it's inevitable that you end up sliding.

One thing I've learned from the OG's from my turf is the art of going O.T. Pimps are constantly on the move 'cause their hoes will get played out if they keep them on the same blade. Plus, after an arrest or two, the police get to know your hoe. That's detrimental for the 'ism. With that schooling the next move was obvious. After pillaging the city for all it had, we had to hit the road. The jig was up. Ha! We raped the 'V' like some Vikings. And the time came for us to search out different horizons.

When the rap game cracked it's doors, me and the cuddies kicked them open like it was a home invasion. We got on that tour circuit and stuck with it full time. Instead of going back to the turf during the week like we were originally doing, we stayed in whatever town Cube's tour bus parked at.

Just 'cause we got serious about touring didn't mean we slowed down with hitting licks though. We stayed hitting shit the whole time. Every once in a while other cuddies would actually meet up with us on the road. People who were square to our movement just saw as a young act trying to pay our dues. It was true, but there was a lot more going on than what the public was seeing. The fact is, we was really deep in the game. Deeper than we had ever been.

We were going hard like our lives depended on it. I still remember that shit like it was yesterday. It was a constant grind. If we weren't performing we was scoping out a spot along the route to hit. Oh yeah, and I can't forget the bitches. The louies were fucking so many breezies it seemed unreal.

Cube actually got at me about that shit one day. In many ways, he was like a big brother to me. This was before we knew what happened to Eazy E so niggaz was indiscriminately fucking on random females. Cube saw how street me and the Cuddies were. That nigga was gutta too. But he was more experienced than the rest of us in a lot of ways. One of the things he told me on this particular day was not to fuck the dancers that travelled with the tour. Back then a tour wasn't a tour without some fly-girls on stage.

I remember Cube saying, "Dre, don't ever fuck none of these bitches we traveling wit'. Fucking the dancers always brings problems. They get jealous, gossip and start fighting with each other. Females got ways of killing the vibe if they don't get they way. I'm telling you, take heed to this game, Dre. Don't fuck with the dancers..."

Each one teach one is a slogan Crestsiders live by, so of course I shared this game with the louies. On some real shit, though; I doubt any of them were listening that day. When it comes to pussy, most niggaz gotta learn from first hand experience.

The tour we was on had two separate buses. There was the one Cube and his immediate circle travelled in. That mothafucka was plushed out with separate rooms. It had everything from TV screens to Fax machines. A sound system and some refrigerators. It was luxurious.

The bus the rest of us pushed in was more like a Greyhound. It had cloth seats, storage areas above the seats and a small restroom in the back. At first, touring on that bus was fun. The energy was inspiring. It was infectious, but shit got tiring after a while though. See, I ain't had no problem pushing with the Cuddies everyday. They was like my brothers. Riding with other mothafuckaz who were sometimes on some weird shit became unbearable. That's why we ended up following the tour in our own rentals. Instead of sleeping on the bus like everybody else we stayed in hotel rooms along the way.

In the beginning I was actually shocked at all the crazy shit I was seeing. Sometimes, I don't think people really feel me when I tell 'em I seen a gang of crazy shit on tour so let me take a little detour for a moment to share with you something I saw one night.

At any given time, there were anywhere from eight to twelve dancers on tour with us. There were two of them that I'll tell you about right now. One was dark skinned girl from Pasadena called Zetia. She was slim and cute, but mean as fuck. The other one was a white girl from Malibu.

It's a trip 'cause back then white girls didn't really have ass like sistahs. This one did though. Her name was Tay. I never really saw either one of them together which is one aspect of why what happened that night always stuck in my mind. We had just did a show in Tacoma, Washington. It was raining pretty hard and we had all been on the road for a minute. Mothafuckaz was tired. Damn near everyone on the bus was knocked out that night. Slumber land for real.

Me, Diggs and Kilo were all on the bus that night. We were all the way in the back next to the restroom. All of us were asleep but something woke me from my sleep in time to see Zetia stepping into the bathroom. I shut my eyes trying to catch that rest before it slipped away but little did I know, my nap time was over.

Tay was seated a few rows up, across the aisle from us. I could see the top of her head as she stared out the window but I really didn't pay her no mind.

A few minutes after Zetia went in, my rest was disrupted again by a faint sound coming from the restroom. At first, I wasn't sure, but it sounded like she was straining. It was like she was tryna take a shit but was having hella-extra problems with that movement. At one point I almost started laughing. It was getting louder and the thought of a bitch having problems shitting was comical to me.

I saw Tay look around. For some reason, I shut my eyes and played possum. Really can't say why. Maybe it was 'cause I felt a little weird listening to a bitch strain like that. So, like I said, Tay looked around, probably trying to see who was up. When nobody stirred, she got up and went to the restroom.

Tap. Tap. Tap.

She tapped on the door and Zetia called out, "Somebody's in here."

"I know, girl," said the white girl. "Let me in real quick."

"I'm busy!"

"Let me in!"

Complete silence.

I damn near held my breath. I didn't want Tay to know I was up. After a few quiet moments passed the door was unlocked and Tay stepped inside. I know y'all know how small them Greyhound restrooms be. Tay couldn't shut the door all the way. The light inside was dim, yet I was able to see in there without being noticed.

I heard Tay ask, "You having problems pooping?"

"Yeah, bitch! I can't shit for nothing in the world!"

"Z, I know this might sound insane, but I can help you poop."

More silence.

Then I heard some whispering. Next, there was movement. I had to sit up to get a better view. Tay had let go of the door, but was still resting in a position where it was hard to see inside unless I repositioned myself. When I finally did get a good view I couldn't believe my eyes. Tay had Zetia doing some crazy shit. She had leaned back, lifted her knees and rested her feet on the wall. Tay was between her legs facing a wide open pussy and ass.

Then Tay asked Zetia, "You ever do butt stuff?"

"Hell naw, bitch!"

"Check this out, girl. If you do butt stuff you learn how to loosen your muscles back there. It'll help you use the bathroom."

Zetia seemed nervous.

"So, what're you saying? If I finger myself I'll be able to shit better?"

"Basically."

"Man, you're crazy!" Zetia tried to put her legs down, but Tay grabbed her thighs propping them on her shoulders.

"Just trust me, Z."

Zetia shook her head in exasperation. "What're you gonna do?"

"Hold on," Tay said.

She took her hoody off and tossed it on the floor. It landed at the bottom of the door which worked in my favor 'cause it made it to where the door couldn't shut all the way.

Zetia propped her feet back up against the wall. Tay squatted down between them. Tay was wearing a white tank top with no bra. Her titties were chunky. Nipples at attention, saluting the situation. If you don't think what I told you thus far is crazy enough, check out what happened next.

Tay stuck her three middle fingers in her mouth. She slobbered all over them mothafuckaz. Then she rubbed Zetia's asshole with them, getting it moist. I couldn't really see shit that good 'cause my position and the fact that I was trying to remain incognito. But I could've sworn Zetia's asshole started puckering. After a while, Tay stuck her middle finger in Zetia's booty.

Tay was taking her time. She kept spitting on Zetia's booty hole. The wetter it got, the deeper she was able to penetrate her. That's when the scene started changing into something else. Zetia looked like she was beginning to enjoy herself. Tay had sped up so much she was getting loud with it.

I saw Zetia close her eyes, lean her head back and say, "Damn, girl... That shit feels good."

Tay didn't reply. She was all business. At one point, she took her fingers out to study them. I guess she was looking for shit. Then, out of nowhere I saw that bitch put half her hand back in her mouth. I was tripping. Nasty-ass-bitch! She got them mothafuckaz sloppy wet then quickly jammed 'em into Zetia's ass without any warning whatsoever. Even I flinched when I saw her do it.

"Oh shit!" Zetia cried out. "Damn, girl! That shit feels good!"

"I bet. Now, I need you to trust me, okay?"

"Do whatever you want, girl."

Man, I couldn't believe my own eyes and ears. I had to wake the cuddies up for that shit. I shook Tay and whispered for Coolio to wake up too.

"Shhh," I told them. "Check this out, y'all."

They were a little groggy at first but they got up and leaned in to watch the show too.

Tay had smashed her face into Zetia's ass and had started tossing her salad like it was an all you can eat buffet. We all watched as she fucked that girl's ass with her tongue. She was married to the movement if you ask me. That nasty bitch was going so hard with it that her face was head-butting Zetia's pussy. She was fucking that girl's ass like her tongue was a dick!

Zetia was just as into it by then. She grabbed Tay's head and started pulling her face back into her hella fast. The slurping and sloshing sounds started getting louder and louder by the moment.

I damn near punched Diggs 'cause he started laughing out loud. The bitches were so caught up in their nasty tryst they didn't even hear him. Another something they didn't pay no mind to was the smell of shit that was floating from Zetia's ass.

"Damn, Tay!" purred Zetia purred. "Fuck this ass, girl. That shit feels good!"

The smacking sound of Tay's mouth on Zetia's ass was getting louder and louder. We even heard the bitch sucking on her ass. And, on top of that, Zetia's moaning was getting louder and louder with each passing moment.

Zetia was beginning to squirm. Her mouth opened while she locked eyes with Tay. Something was percolating and we could all see it coming.

"Girl, I gotta fart!"

"Okay," Tay replied.

"You're probably ready now. Spread your legs and push. As a matter of fact, hold up. Let me spread your butt cheeks."

I was shaking my mothafuckin' head when I heard that nasty-ass shit. The cuddies all looked at me, tripping! They was just as shocked as me.

Zetia did as she was told. She pushed and we all heard a loud-ass, "Brrr! Brrr! Brrr!"

On God, that shit stank! When I tell you that shit stunk, I mean it smelled like death! It was pure, unadulterated shit fumes coming out that bathroom! Needless to say, the cuddies had enough of that shit. We all started grabbing our shit so we could move towards the front of the bus, as far away from the smell as possible.

Curt was hot! Bruh got up and went to the restroom door, opened it wide then slammed that bitch shut hella hard!

Then he yelled, "Nasty-ass, bitches!"

The whole bus woke up when he did that. Within minutes all the windows were open and the cabin was freezing.

I'm not sure whose idea it was but we didn't stay on that bus that night. The whole bus smelled like shit. We went straight to the driver and told him to stop the mothafucka. We didn't give a fuck that it was raining. We wanted off that bus right then and there.

The driver couldn't take it either. He pulled off the highway at the next exit. Luckily, there was a cheap motel located right off the highway. Me and the louies stayed there that night and got a rental the next morning. After that night, we never rode the bas again. We stayed in rentals and slept at hotels and motels along the way...

CHAPTER

EIGHTEEN

"That's when we got serious. The sticks came out..."
-Mac Dre

A certain sense of melancholy materializes when you look back on things that already took place. It comes from already knowing how things turned out. But when you're in the trenches and shit is moving super fast, there's times you miss the most obvious signs. One of the things I've learned about life is that people rarely, truly get blindsided. Especially when they're dealing with haters.

While growing up, your teachers are everywhere. A teacher can be anybody. A parent, sibling, friends or anyone around you. This is how you learn the rules of your culture. Don't ever think the moves you make are totally originated by yourself. Naw, cuddy. The world doesn't work like that.

Everything you do, whether it's the way you talk, walk or act it's all learned behavior. Even the things you get mad at is dictated by the ways of the people around you. Now, the one aspect of life you're truly in control of is the way you react to whatever situation you're in. Other than that, your moves are basically a mirror of the world around you. That's just how we're wired.

For instance, when you grow up in an active environment you're taught early on that snitching is unacceptable. You don't only see it in the movies, you hear it in the music you listen to. Even your parents will tell you not to snitch on your brothers and sisters. So, we all know snitching ain't cool.

When a McGraw takes you into an alley and offers to let you go if you tell on somebody - it's on the individual to make the decision of whether she's gonna tell or not. Some niggaz keep it stitch-lipped. Some niggaz catch diarrhea of the mouth. Whether one choose to or not, everyone knows it's wrong to tell. Since snitching has been consciously implanted in most of our minds as being wrong, the people who tell on shit will subconsciously tell on themselves. They'll let clues surface to the people around them that they can't be trusted.

The clues may be subtle like not being able to look at you in the eyes, or more direct like making slick ass comments. You just gotta pay attention and you can catch it on most occasions.

If you look closely you can catch when people telegraph their guilty conscious. Most of the time, if you get snitched on it's by someone you know. It's usually someone close. Someone in your circle. And, nine times outta ten if it's someone around you, you'll be able to sniff 'em out.

For the sake of moving this story along I purposely left out some of the incidents that took place when the Crest was at it's hottest with Johnny Law. Even after we hit the road, Twelve kept coming through the hood. They wasn't just driving through either. They was aggressive with their tactics. They'd park a marked car smack dab in the middle of a track, shutting down dope spots. They were picking up prostitutes and locking them up for no reason. They were going to cuddy's houses harassing our mommas and grannys. I'm serious when I say it was like war.

Meanwhile, you had niggaz like me who was sticking and moving. We was still hitting shit while the turf was getting raped by them crackas. We didn't let what they were doing humble us. We was still flossing on the whole city. When the turf was at its hottest me, Kilo, Diggs, Unda Dogg and Mall were still hitting corners in Beemers, Benzes, and old school muscle cars on shiny thangs.

I'm not going to name anyone in particular right now. It's not like there was only one individual snitching. The 'hood was way too hot and the police had their mind made up that the Romper Room was behind all the robberies. Add that in with the fact that our rap careers had the spotlight on us in a major way and you had a recipe for disaster. Still, we dived in head first not caring about the consequences.

Basically, it was a cuddy who wore a wire for the Feds. The snitch nigga was in the room talking to the cuddies about a job and that's what got the Alphabet boys involved. I know who it was. And I'm telling you, there were times when I'd catch the fuck-nigga looking away 'cause he couldn't look me in the eyes. He even made a comment or two disguised as a joke to the guise that me and the louies weren't letting anyone else eat. It was bullshit, but it was clue on top of clue that this nigga was on some rodent shit. We were all just moving too fast to catch the crumbs he kept leaving behind.

So, back to the tour. After we stopped riding the bus with everyone else we suddenly had a lot more freedom to move around. Most of the shows were held on the weekends so we always had the whole week to bounce around and chill. By "we" I mean me, Curt, Diggs, Unda Dogg and sometimes Mall.

It was one of the best times of my life. I had money... we all had money and bitches. What made it so smooth was the tour would take us through a city and give us just the right amount of time to case out a bank and hit it. We might make a cool ten G's off a show along with another twenty from a bank. Then turn around and invest a chunk of it into studio time.

The cuddies all felt like I was gonna take us to the next level so we all invested in my projects. That type of shit only works when you pushing with real niggaz who have a lifetime of trust and loyalty built up.

On this particular week Diggs had met some sexy-ass Mexican girls who was with the business. I had just did a show in Fresno the weekend before so them niggaz had already peeped out a lick for us.

Fresno had a big Bank of America down town. It sat on a single lot with a large parking lot and two entrances. It was the same set up as our first Bank heist in the *V*. It just looked perfect and it really would've been if the Feds wouldn't have been following us!

We was in Fresno for about three days. The first day was all partying. We went and picked up the bitches and took 'em to the Holiday Inn where we had three different rooms all connected. The drinks and the drugs was flowing all while them bad-ass long haired Chicano bitches was running through all three rooms butt-ass naked!

The second day we went out to check on the lick. I'm telling you the bank sat nice. We already had an extra car because one of the girls was letting Diggs push her whip. Everything was Gucci. It was all set up.

It was agreed that I was gonna sit that one out. I was doing them shows and they had me sitting on racks so I really didn't need the money like the cuddies did. The plan was that the cuddies were gonna park around the corner from the bank. They planned to walk up to the bank, hit it then jog back to the getaway vehicle. After hitting a few corners they'd ditch that car then get into Diggs ride and come pick me up from the room.

Another reason I had to sit that one out was because the females knew exactly who I was. The cuddies had given them hoes fake names an all that so they were straight.

That's one of the major perks of going OT. People you deal with only know what you tell them. There's never a need to tell anyone anything real about yourself. And, as long as they don't ever know anything authentic about you then they can't tell the Law shit that's worth anything.

The night before that lick was one night I'll never forget. It was perfect. If you ever been with your cuddies and all of you have money, new clothes, big pistols and a gang of hoes then you know exactly how we all felt that night. The music was banging. The bitches was dancing and laughing, having a good time. Blunts weren't even in rotation because they didn't need to be. All the Cuddies had their own blunts. We played dice. Ordered big Chinese food. Even invited the delivery nigga in and took his money off his whack-ass dice game. At the end of the night, when it was time to settle in we all had two hoes a piece!

The next morning, after getting rid of the females we got right down to business. That's when we got serious. The sticks came out. Diggs had the compact Mac 10 and Curt had the Dirty Hairy .44. Since our first few licks we learned to control them trigger fingers. A professional robber doesn't go into a juxt with violence on his mind. All we want is the money. So it wasn't as if the cuddies was carrying with the intent of creating chalk lined silhouettes.

That's actually one of the benefits of hitting banks. They not like moms and pops spots where the person you're robbing is so invested in the money you're taking that they might put their life on the line to keep it. Bank employees are actually trained to hand over the bread because it's federally insured. At the same time, that's the catch though. Once you hit one that's federally protected you playing in the big leagues 'cause them Alphabet boys get involved and they got way more training and resources than the regular police. What we didn't know at the time was we were being followed the whole time. The Feds had followed us all the way from Vallejo to Fresno.

Since I sat that one out it was on me to make sure I had everything ready to go by the time they came back and got me. It's not like we had bags or anything. We had so much money, niggaz just bought clothes when our old shit got dirty. At least, that's how we pushed when we was OT.

On our last day, which wasn't supposed to be the last day the Cuddies were 'posed to hit the lick then we were going to get another room at another spot. We were gonna party one more night with the girls we had been with the night before. But things didn't go down as planned. About an hour after the Cuddies left they came back trippin'...

Boom! Boom! Boom! sounded the door.

When I yelled, "Who is it?" The cuddy replied, "It's us, cuddy! Let us in!"

Something was wrong. Something was most definitely wrong.

I opened the door and they came in all wide eyed.

"C'mon, Dre!" Diggs started. "We gotta go!"

"What's wrong?" I asked sensing a dilemma at hand.

"C'mon, Dre! We'll explain in the car," Curt demanded.

In less than five minutes we were on the freeway headed towards the Bay. By then, I had already figured something went wrong with the robbery. I just didn't know exactly what happened yet.

"Cuddy," Curt started from the front passenger seat. "They was on us!"

"What'chu mean?" I asked. "Did you hit the lick, or what?"

"No!" Diggs replied. "As soon as we got there we saw three news vans. One on each side of the bank and the other one across the street."

"Cuddy," Curt said. "Them crackas was everywhere. They were tryna get the news vans to leave. It's like they knew we was coming!"

"How y'all know they was there for you?"

Diggs was clearly spooked. Every few seconds he'd glance at the rearview mirror. The ride was filled with tension. The vibe was nothing like it had been that morning or the day before. Shit was ominous.

Then Curt blurted out, "Y'all see that Crown Vic' back there?"

"Which one?" Diggs asked. "The blue one?"

"Yeah. That mothafucka was at the bank!"

"Man, y'all trippin'!" I said, hoping I was right. But, on some real shit I knew it wasn't a false alarm because my niggaz was professionals. Never once had any of them been on some random paranoid shit. Even when we was kids, it never happened like that. So, I was basically just trying to calm them down.

"Dre!" Curt said. "We not trippin', Mac! They knew we was coming. I don't know how, but they knew."

That's when we all heard the ghetto bird swooping around above us.

"See!" Diggs exclaimed. "That's a news helicopter right there!"

"Fuck!" we all said.

That's when it happened!

They blitzed.

The sirens sounded. Unmarked cars with red and blue lights in their grills serenaded the chase.

Fuck!

We all knew the protocol. If the law ever gets behind you it's all gas, no brakes. If anything, a chase will give you time to get rid of your heaters. The problem was we were in the middle of nowhere! We was just outside of a town called Los Banos, a small farming town in Central California.

Like I said… the middle of nowhere.

"What y'all wanna do?" Diggs asked us.

"Shit," I started. "Y'all didn't even go up in the bank, right?"

"Then the most they gonna get us for is these guns."

Kilo spoke up, "I'll take the guns, cuddy. Just bail me out and pay for the lawyer."

"You sure?" I asked him.

"On 3 C's. I'll just end up with some probation. Ain't no bodies on 'em. I'll be good."

I looked at Diggs, "You cool with that, cuddy?"

"If that's what the louie wants to do."

"Here," demanded Curt. "Give me the straps. When they pull us out, all the guns'll be on me…"

CHAPTER NINETEEN

"The shenanigans started immediately.
They didn't take us straight to jail."
-Mac Dre

Jay pulled over on the side of that deserted stretch of highway and we were immediately surrounded by the law. They made a full spectacle of it too. Ghetto bird in the sky. Unmarked cars everywhere. The whole nine. Then, as if the day couldn't get any worse, I heard the last voice I would have ever wanted to hear in a situation like that.

After the guy behind the bullhorn had me and the Cuddies get out the ride he told us to kneel down and interlock our fingers behind our heads. Next thing I heard was, "I got this one!"

I turned my head to verify what my ears were telling me and I saw McGraw heading straight towards me.

"Turn your fucking head around, Dre!"

"What-da-fuck!" Kilo said. "This shit gotta be illegal!"

"Ha!" McGraw gloated. "We finally got you dumb-ass motherfuckers! We been following you for the last three days!"

McGraw slapped the cuffs on me hella rough and disrespectful like. Then he stood me up and lead me to the back of a black on black unmarked police car.

"You know this illegal, right!" I said. "This ain't your jurisdiction-"

"We got weapons!" a pig announced.

Next thing I know, they was forcing the cuddies into the back of a van. They were cussing them pigs out, but it didn't matter. They had us. Still, I was hot! I leaned back and booted the fuck outta the window closest to me.

Boom! Boom! Boom!

"Fuck y'all pigs!" I yelled.

The door came open.

I was dragged out.

Someone socked me in the mouth. Someone else kicked me in the ribs. Then stank-breath McGraw crouched down next to me and said, "I got you, Dre. I got the whole fucking Romper Room! It's over, cuddy!"

After that, I was thrown into the van the louies were in.

"You a'ight, cuddy?" the asked me.

My mouth was busted. My ribs hurt. My shoes were scuffed up. "I'm good. They ain't do shit. What about y'all?"

"We good," Curt said. "But, Dre."

"Yeah."

"They ain't VPD. This is the Feds, cuddy."

"Naw!" I replied. "McGraw-"

"Look at they windbreakers, cuddy," Diggs said. "That's dem boys..."

I took a good look out the van's back windows and saw the letters FBI embossed on their jackets. That's when I knew it was all bad.

$$$$$

The shenanigans started immediately. They didn't take us straight to jail. At first, that's where I thought they were taking us. I couldn't have been more wrong. They took us to the Federal building in downtown Fresno.

It was all business with them folks. Anytime I've been arrested, the booking process was long and fucked up. Them folks didn't waste no time. We were all split up from the moment we were taken out the van. At the time I didn't know where they took Diggs and Kilo. All I knew was I was parked in a dreary room with a table and a two-way mirror. It reminded me of that interrogation room on Law and Order where the pigs talk their suspects into telling on themselves.

They had me in that room for less than five minutes before a Black mothafucka in street clothes came in with some folders in his hand. He looked like a clean cut street nigga. Other than the FBI ID card hanging from his neck I would've thought he was a normal nigga.

"How you doing, Mr. Hicks?" he asked me as he sat down. One of his folders was nonchalantly placed in front of me. The other one stayed in front of him.

I didn't reply to his dumb-ass question. Not only was I trained to stay stitch-lipped, I was still fuming from the ass whooping I had just received on the side of the highway.

He didn't need a reply though. He went ahead with his spiel. "I need you to really listen to what I'm about to tell you right now. Andre... I understand how angry you are right now. But I need you to clear your head because the decisions you choose to make over the next thirty minutes will dictate the outcome of the rest of your life."

I raised an eyebrow at the Uncle Tom then shook my head. I swear I don't know where they find these mothafuckaz. *Dictate the outcome of the rest of my life...*

Hmph!

"I know you're a rapper, Andre. Your career is blowing up. Anyone with half a brain can see that. You're doing shows with Ice Cube. Taking your peeps along for the ride. You're on your way up, my boy."

He stopped speaking for a minute. Probably thinking I was gonna say something.

Silence.

"Open the folder, Dre."

Now I was *Dre*. This guy was a joke! I didn't budge.

"Here, I'll open it for you."

He opened the folder and spread a gang of pictures across the table. The images were of me, Diggs and Kilo over the previous several days. He even had some pictures that really threw me for a loop. There were pictures of us *inside* the hotel room with the bitches!

The majority of the pictures I saw were of all three of us casing the bank though. To me, it wasn't shit. None of that was proof of shit 'cause we hadn't done anything.

He must've seen me looking at the hotel room pictures too long 'cause he said, "Yeah. The women you were kicking it with over the weekend are Federal informants. They're from Oregon working to knock time off their uncle's prison term.

"Oh! Ha!" he laughed. "You thought it was a game? Dre, we don't play. We're the FBI. You've been on our radar for months. You couldn't think you could hit banks and getaway-"

"Look, man! I don't know what kind of bullshit McGraw been feeding y'all. But we don't rob banks! We rap! I got paycheck stubs to prove what I do. you can dismiss me wit' the bullshit and let me call a bondsman 'cause I'm done here."

"Bond! Ha-ha-ha!" That really tickled that bitch. "Hicks, you're under Federal Indictment. You can't have a bond, but you can get an OR."

"What?!"

"Dre, listen closely. We are charging you and the louies, as you guys call yourselves, with thirteen different robberies. Where it stands now, I have the leeway to hit you with lesser charges if you cooperate. It's too late for your friends. They're getting charged with the actual robberies. But, you. I can charge you with conspiracy if you talk to me. And trust me when I tell you it's a lot less than what they got coming. I can give you my word you can get out today."

"Today?"

"Yup. You'll be back on the road with Ice Cube tonight."

I couldn't believe that nigga. Sitting there talking to me like what he was saying made sense.

"So, you ready?"

"Ready? Man, suck my diiick!"

He shook his head and said, "Dre, you are the star here. If you ride out this fake-ass gangster routine your whole career will go down in flames before it really gets started. I can get you out today. You can walk out that door a free man. And, if you're afraid your boyz will smutt your name up, you got nothing to worry about. We got ways of silencing people for years at a time.

"You's a bitch! Get me the fuck outta here!"

He didn't budge. Instead, he opened the folder that was sitting in front of him. There were pictures in that one too. He picked up the first one and held it up for me to see.

"You know her?"

It was a picture of my homegirl, Rene. It was a trip to see her image, but I didn't say anything. He tossed the one picture in front of me then picked up another photo and held it up for me to see. This one had Kilo and Coolio in a rental. He tossed that one towards me and picked up another one. The next one had Rene in the car with them. He tossed that one in front of me before picking up another one. Now, he was holding one up of all three of them entering a hotel room together. The following six or seven flicks were blurry. Someone had snuck up to their window and took pictures of the inside of the motel room through a crack in the curtains.

I wasn't sure where he was going with what he was showing me. Rene was a ripper. We all went to school together.

"So, I take it you know Rene Sherbert."

Silence.

I was starting to get confused but I didn't show any emotions.

"I know she's your girlfriend, Dre."

"What?!"

I had no idea where this bitch was getting his intel, but he couldn't have been more wrong. Rene was a homegirl from the turf.

"Here's your main guys fucking your girl, Dre. After seeing these pictures you shouldn't have no reason to be loyal to them. They're obviously not loyal to you."

Now it was time to really act a fool! This idiot was on some real dumb shit. Plus, I reasoned, if he thought Rene was my bitch, then he really didn't know shit about any of us. He was a fucking idiot!

"Get me the fuck outta here! Fuck you! Fuck McGraw! Fuck a bank! The cuddies don't rob banks, bitch!" I was yelling extra loud by then. "Fuck what you talking 'bout, pig!"

Bam!

I was caught in mid sentence by a loud thump on the two way mirror. A few seconds later, McGraw came in through the door. He was heading straight towards me like he was gonna get on me or something.

"You little motherfucker! I know you! You're a piece of shit!"

"What the hell! Get the hell out of here!" the Fed yelled.

McGraw was coming at me, but Uncle Tom wasn't having it. He tackled 'im, slamming that honky against the wall before he could get to me.

Suddenly, the room was filled with cops. All of them had the look of law enforcement even though none of them were in uniform.

"Get this dumb son-of-a--bitch out of here now!" the Uncle Tom yelled furiously. They ended up dragging McGraw's dumb-ass up outta of there like the piece of shit he was!

Uncle Tom took one last look at me and then told one of his cronies, "We're done here." He looked back at me after that and said, "Hicks, this isn't a game. We aren't like that Neanderthal who just came in here. He's ignorant. He's never going to amount to shit. He's an uneducated racist who shouldn't have a badge. But that's neither he nor there. The bottom line is if you don't give me something you're gonna end up spending the next thirty years of your life in a prison cell."

I stared at him for a cool ten seconds before I said, "Take me to jail..."

The next few hours were a blur. I was hot! I couldn't believe they had the audacity to approach me with some snitch shit. When they finally took me to the Fresno County jail I was booked in alone. The cuddies were nowhere in sight. Later on, it came out that they were taken straight to the county. They weren't questioned or propositioned like I was.

Snitching was never an option. However, that night as the deputies took their sweet time booking me I thought about everything Uncle Tom had said. It was unbelievable. First of all, I grew up with my Romper Room niggaz. Through the good and bad times, we experienced everything together. We never once left a cuddy for dead. At the time, telling on a cuddy to get oneself out of trouble was unheard of. We just didn't operate like that. Plus, I'm a gangsta'. When I agree to move on anything I make it my duty to become fully aware of all the risks that're involved. I'm a realest. Growing up in the ghetto exposed me to the good, the bad and the ugliness of the game. Since I know all of what comes with it, what I look like telling on a Cuddy? It's not an option.

CHAPTER TWENTY

*"My album IN DA HOOD was recorded while
I was fighting that Fed case."*
-Mac Dre

If we would've gotten arrested at home they would've sent us to the Solano County Jail in Fairfield. Since that's not how it went down, we ended up in Fresno.

Fresno's county lockup is way bigger than ours. The internal political structure between the inmates is different too.

In our county jail Three C's runs shit. We got a strong presence on every floor and in every pod. We're not the only faction to push in the county but we are at the top of the food chain. In Fresno the structure was different mostly because they had gangs pushing a line. The VPD will tell you the Romper Room is a gang, in many ways we are. But we're not like Bloods, Crips, Bulldogs, Northeners or Southerners. We don't carry bandannas, or do drive-byes. We pimp hoes and do walk-ups.

They didn't take me to the pod where I was to be housed at until the next morning. By then the cuddies were already settled in. We had a Romper Room huddle as soon as I came in and saw them in the dayroom. For the most part, it felt just like any other time we all ended up locked up together.

I think I slept for most of the first week. The streets were good to a nigga so I had missed a lot of rest. Once I got that out my system it was time to get into the routine of county jail life. To pass time we played cards, dominoes, dice and read books. I read a lot of books. Other than that, we ran that phone line up.

The phone was really the main event because it was a portal to the streets. Me and the louies kept that wall phone in rotation. The only problem was there wasn't enough phones in that bitch. They had us housed in a pod that had two tiers. It housed 48 inmates and we all had to share three phones!

One of the first things I noticed about that county jail that was different than our county jail was the politics. Fresno was known for it's city-wide gang called Bulldogs. They're a Mexican gang whose numbers are extremely high based on the fact that their whole county was their territory. Damn near every Hispanic male between the ages of 14 to 40 was a Bulldog. They outnumbered the Blacks two to one. This meant they had a strong say on how things were ran in each pod.

Me, Kilo and Diggs were from the Bay area. This made us aliens. The masses seemed to love us, but fame only took you so far when get thrown into captivity. The rules change. It's no longer about fame and clout. It's about your hands and your heart.

If you haven't noticed it by now, let me clarify something real quick: I'm a Crest Side representa'. I'm hyper and fly. Everything I do from my stunnaz to my shoes is hella extra. And all my cuddies are cut from this exact same imported clothe. It really doesn't matter where they put any of us. We go dumb everywhere we go and some people don't like that.

When you're a shiner not all the attention you attract is beneficial. Sometimes, in Cali, when you don't bang, a banger might misconstrue your 'ism. This forces you to flex a few times to demonstrate the seriousness of your push. This took place early on in our stay at that county jail.

Peep the scenario: Each pod had three phones. The rules were set up where two of the phones were for the Mexicans. The extra one was delegated to the Blacks. It didn't even matter what the population was, the Bulldogs had it set up that way.

There's no universe I can imagine where this setup will work for me. Especially not if I'm in attendance. The convict rules were established where even if one of the phones weren't being used they still couldn't be used by another race.

Real talk, that phone was a nigga's lifeline. Between me and the louies we had twelve different bitches who went dumb if we didn't call 'em on a daily basis. And that didn't even include other people we had to call like family and business associates.

We had to squable up for that phone a few times. In the beginning it was hectic 'cause Diggs and Curt were just as hyphy as me and neither one of us was going for that bullshit they was talking. A nigga wasn't about to stand by and watch an empty phone just sit there when we had to get ahold of somebody. It just wasn't gonna happen.

The louies and I grew up together. We had been through hell and back together. There was no way in the world would any of us sit back and watch another one of us lose a fight, either. We might let you get a fair one, but losing wasn't an option. It didn't matter what the odds were, a nigga wasn't gonna whoop a cuddy on my watch. So, yeah, we knuckled up a few times before shit got established in our favor.

When it was all said and done, that third phone got shared. It was worth it, too 'cause we had real life business to handle. Niggaz wasn't on some cup caking shit.

Something I never understood was how much time niggaz wasted on them stress boxes. Don't get me wrong, them phones is tapped. You gotta be aware of that. However, that doesn't mean you should use it on bullshit. I watched upper echelon niggaz with machines come through that Federal lockup. And the way some of them pushed was blasphemous.

I've watched a few niggaz who got locked up and changed right before my eyes. At first they be on some gangsta shit, barking orders at they bitches. Then, after the weeks and months go by those same *fellaz* turn into suckaz for they bitch. They start worrying 'bout what they punk-rock bitch is doing instead of establishing who's 'posed to take over their machine.

I couldn't do it like that. Fuck a bitch, cuddy. That phone was my line to the streets. When I did talk to a breezy it was to send her on a mission. I ended up recording a whole album over that county jail phone. My album *IN DA HOOD* was recorded while I was fighting that Fed case.

They kept me in that bitch a whole year. That bitch-ass Uncle Tom was on some bullshit when he threw them football numbers at me. I pled out to five years at 85%. But the one thing he was right about was that it put my career on hold.

Me and the louies were penitentiary rich. None of us ever went hungry. It wasn't enough to sustain my career though. When I was out, we all reinvested our money into the music. Paying for videos, studio time, and album pressing helped push the 3 C's movement. The extracurricular money really helped for real! Not only that, the shows was where the legal money came through in bags. Even after splitting it with the team, the shows still kept us fed.

The problem is, you can't do shows from lock-up. And what's that old adage?

Out of sight, out of mind...

CHAPTER
TWENTY ONE

"I stumbled, yet didn't fall."
-Mac Dre

When you're as young as I was when I caught my time you really don't have a full grasp on time. Considering the scope of a whole lifetime, five years really isn't that long. I know that now, but there's no way I was gonna understand that when the judge gave me my time. To me, five years seemed like a life sentence.

My first stop in the federal prison system was Lompoc. Lompoc is an old Federal penitentiary. A reception center for Federal inmates who catch their cases on the West Coast. The moment I got off the van was one of awakening. It was my first time in the big house and all I had to go by were second hand stories told by older convicts. No matter how vivid of an account they gave a nigga, none of it prepared me for the world I was about to enter.

Since me and the louies all took our plea deals on the same day, we also hit Lompoc on the same day. It wasn't like everywhere else we did time together at though. They separated us from the jump. We all got housed in different buildings.

Before I continue, it's important that I clarify some things. Most people, when they think of the Federal Bureau of Prisons, think of something called "Club Fed." They think of golf courses, tennis games and swimming pools. Get that out your mind right now. Some of the most violent individuals in this country are housed in the Federal prison system. There's just as many riots, stabbings and murders as any level 4 prison in the State of California.

I'll never forget the first full fledged riot I was in. It was during a morning yard. It was cold-as-fuck out there. They only gave us yard three times a week, so it really didn't matter how bad the weather was, a nigga had to go out. Imagine a low budget park with a baseball field and two basketball courts. All of it encircled by twenty-foot cement walls. Ain't no getting over the walls without a helicopter or ladder. And even if you happened to fall upon either of those things - the sharp shooters in the towers would be on some Blocka-Blocka shit.

The yard was split up by invisible borders created by the prison politics. Every race had it's own territory and crossing those borders could get you fucked up real quick.

When I first got there, they put me in the cell by myself. This limited me when it came to obtaining certain information. For instance, I really didn't know where to go when they ran yard. That didn't really matter, though. As soon as I hit the yard I headed straight towards the basketball courts. I don't care where they put you, the basketball courts will always be a universal gathering spot for all Blacks.

So it was my first time hitting the yard and I immediately felt something wasn't right. Anna was in the air something drastic. You ain't gotta be a seasoned convict to recognize tension in the air. Your natural senses will automatically warn you when there's a threat in the mix.

There were at least eight to nine hundred people on the yard that morning. Yet, the yard seemed empty. Kinda empty if that makes sense. As I looked around I noticed that all the Blacks were grouped up on the court, but no one was playing ball. The whites were in another section of the yard, and so were the Mexicans. Everyone was huddled up.

Even though it was my first time walking that yard, no one could've told me what I was experiencing was business as usual.

"Hey! You Dre?" a young nigga about my age asked me a few moments after I approached the crowd huddled up on the basketball court.

"Who're you?" I asked defensively.

"I'm Shark from Stockton. Check it out, bruh. I know who you are. I fucked with your music on the streets. But we ain't got time for all that right now. There's static on the yard with another race. If it kicks off, you rockin'?"

"I don't think I got a choice."

"You right," he smirked. "Take this."

He handed me a sharp piece of metal about as thick as a pen. There was a shoe lace tied around one end of it for a handle. I quickly tucked it in my waistband and acted like nothing was going on.

"See them Mecs over there?" he asked me while looking towards the southern end of the yard where the baseball field was located. It looked like a million Mexicans were having a pow-wow. The real count had to have been around five-hundred though.

Someone a few feet from us asked out loud, "What's the count?"

Someone else replied, "Two-hundred-sixty Mexicans. Eighty-seven Africans."

Then the brother who gave me the piece told me, "Chances are, it's 'bout to crack, bruh."

"Why?"

"I can't tell you 'cause I don't even know. It could be a debt, or some sort of disrespect. The tension just showed up this morning."

Right before I could ask another question the yard's vibe went from 60 to 100. The crowd around us started moving forward, causing me to look around to see why.

A wave of Mexicans were heading towards us at a fast pace. Half of them had weapons and none of them looked like they were coming to talk.

It's a trip how that *fight or flight* instinct works. There's an automatic reaction when faced with a threat. It's natural and it's root lies within your natural urge to survive. That morning, every single African on that basketball court chose to fight.

"Stay close!" barked Shark.

"Got'chu, cuddy!"

The yard went up! It was like a scene out of some sort of Aztec movie. People were fighting all around me. The coldness of the air didn't matter any more since everyone was Stanley Steaming.

I stabbed the first person that got within arms reach of me. I wasn't playing. They had weapons, big metal shit. Ya' boy got hands though.

I'm known for knocking niggaz out. But I'll be damned if I bring knuckles to a knife fight!

So, I stuck one of them then I went at another one. Next thing I knew, three of them ran towards me from my left and right sides. My new nigga, Shark had my back though. He knocked one of them smooth out before going at another one with his piece. That helped, but they started coming from everywhere. All I could do was stick and move as best as I could. I was getting socked the fuck up from all sides but I kept fighting. Then came the thunder!

Bladadah! Bladadah! Bladadah!

Boom! Boom! Boom!

Shots fired! Concussion grenades exploded. Smoke bombs filled the field with clouds of burning smoke. Some of us were suddenly disorientated. The yard was a war zone.

"Dre! Dre!" Shark yelled.

"Yeah!" I replied through the fog.

"Take ya' shirt off and do this!" Shark ripped his shirt off and wrapped it around his face like a ninja mask. I did the same.

Just as I was trying to tie a knot behind my head, somebody hit me on the side of my head. I stumbled but stayed on my feet. My next punch hit its mark, knocking a paisa clean out! I was dazed. I couldn't breathe or see shit! Through the fog, like twenty yards away I could've sworn I seen some opps swarm an old man. They had the brotha' and were literally dragging him towards their side of the yard.

"Shark! Check it out!" I yelled while pointing in their direction.

As soon as he saw what I was pointing at he didn't have to say anything. We both started running in their direction. Several other Africans followed us and we attacked their line of defense. I dropped my piece along the way. But a lot of other people did as well. We got swarmed. It was shoulder to shoulder fisticuffs!

Boom! Boom! Boom! Blasted the A.R. 15!

Two Mexicans dropped!

I froze.

Shark didn't. He had a Mec on the ground. He was on top of him, stabbing that mothafucka nonstop! I don't know what made me look up at the tower but I did. I saw a cop getting ready to take his shot.

"Sharrr-"

Boom!

Shark's head exploded! It happened right in front of me. Everyone froze. A few more bombs were tossed causing background noise. But nothing was as loud and shocking as the shot that killed Shark.

Suddenly, pigs in riot gear came from everywhere. The riot had ended just as quick as it started. And, that was my initiation in to the Federal prison system...

CHAPTER
TWENTY-TWO

*"Since I turn it up no matter where I go,
there's not a prison on Earth that can dim my glow."*
-Mac Dre

There's no one there to hold your hand in prison. I've seen the hardest men break, while some soft niggaz grew nuts and became men. Although, that was the first time I saw some shit like that, it wouldn't be the last. Prison is a serious place with no room for mistakes.

That riot showed me that niggaz in the joint were playing for keeps. Mothafuckaz got stabbed, stomped out and shot. From that day on, I made sure I kept a makeshift tucked away for war times. Lompoc taught me that.

One of the most obvious differences between doing time in the Feds over State is they can send you to the other side of the country if they want to. I was lucky to do all my time at Lompoc because it was on the West Coast. It kept me close to the house. Not everyone that goes to the Feds gets blessed like that, though. One of my cuddies went to Fire Camp out here in Cali. It was close to home, no walls or nothing. But he started fucking up and they ended up sending him to a prison in North Carolina. He couldn't see his family because he was on the other side of the country. Them bitches play a cold game.

The B.O.P. loves shipping niggaz to Michigan, where it snows so hard you gotta hold on to a rope to get from building to building. That mothafucka snows like Siberia! It be so cold, don't nobody wanna fight. On top of that, it's so far away from home you end up losing contact with most of your loved ones.

When you have a bunch of men who have thirty, forty or fifty years and they have no contact with their loved ones, it creates a whole different atmosphere. There's an "I don't give a fuck" attitude about everything. They don't have anything to lose since everything has already been taken away. When you're in the midst of that type of shit, you have to man up real quick.

I only had five years to do. Even though I thought five years was a life sentence, it really wasn't. I also had royalties from my music money coming in. Add that in with the fact that I stayed in California and it made my time more easier than what it could've been otherwise.

I met real mob figgaz throughout my time in prison. There were niggaz who actually touched millions. On the streets they were famous but after going away, the streets they left them for dead. I recognized that shit real quick. It was something I couldn't afford to let happen to me though. My career wasn't over. The streets were still in store for me. So I fought hard to stay in touch with them.

Since I turn it up no matter where I go there's not a prison on earth that can dim my glow. This got me caught up a few times throughout my time. But what can I say? Mac Dre gonna do Mac Dre no matter where I'm at. Point blank!

After reception, the administration moved me to another part of the prison. A section separated from reception. It was the yard where inmates actually served out their bids. There, I was housed with people who had been there for years so they were established.

Once I got settled in, my time got a little easier. I'm never gonna say I had fun in prison. Fuck the B.O.P.! I wouldn't wish captivity on my worst enemy. Yet, on some real shit, I made my environment as comfortable as possible.

My cell was always plushed out. There were rugs on the floor. Pictures of bitches on the walls. A boom-box that rumbled the cell like there were twelves under the bunk. I stayed on the phone. Back then, not a lot of niggaz had cell phones, but I had access to the State phone and I stayed on it. I also went to store every month. The cell stayed with zoom-zooms and wham-whams. Not to mention the fact that I stayed stealing shit out the kitchen once I got a job in there. Ya' boy was on some penitentiary rich shit.

Some people call the visitation room *The dance floor*. They call it that 'cause you show up with your girl dressed in your best. It's when you couple up and cupcake the whole day. I stayed in that visitation room. Something about me is the Crest raised me to be a real player. By no means was any of my bitches handcuffed when I was locked up. I always had fun with every female who ever came to see me. Plus, having bitches come see me kept me connected to the streets.

Let me tell y'all something I learned throughout that time. This is about women and the impact they have on the world around us. When I first got involved in the music industry all my work was on some gangsta' shit. I was rapping for all the niggaz who were in the streets like me and my Cuddies. Somewhere along the line I realized something. I realized that most niggaz do what they do to impress bitches. When females think something is popping, then niggaz will follow that because everything revolves around impressing the women.

When I figured that out, I started paying attention to women a lot more. I went from staying in a bitch ear to listening to what comes out her mouth. That's how I stayed up to date with what was happening on the turf.

When ecstasy first started circulating a lot of niggaz in prison didn't have any idea what it was, or how the high felt. Not me. I was on that shit while I was in captivity. The first time I tried it, I got it from the homegirl, Fidae. Fidae was from the V but she was Spanish. She was turnt up all the time and I loved vibing with her.

Fidae used to come see me all the time. Well, this one time she came through, I came into the visitation room and there was a gang of candy waiting for me on the table. She had already raided the vending machine before I got out there. As soon as I sat down she told me to eat everything except the Skittles. Baby had me drinking a gang of Orange juice too. At first, I didn't realize why she was on what she was on, but in the end I found out there was a method to her madness. She kept telling me she had some *new shit* in the Skittles.

Fidae had brought me in some weed and coke before so it wasn't new to me to get a party pack from her. But that time she was acting funny. Funny in a good way. She was acting like she had brought me some shit that was on a different level. She built it up so much that I couldn't wait to get back to the unit so I could try it out.

At the time, I was in the cell with my nigga, Paperboy. PB was from Pittsburgh, California. A small, but turnt' up city in the Bay Area.

Neither one of us had done X before. All we had to go off was what we and heard about it. That it intensified whatever vibe you was in when you did it. If you on some drill shit, your 'ism gonna be animalistic. If you take it when you on some party shit, it'll have you going dumb! With that info imbedded in my mental, me and PB came up with a plan. We decided to get into a good mood before getting on it. We got a quart of whiskey, rolled up some trees and turned the music up. We had that cell banging like an old school bending corners through the Bay!

Then, right when we started feeling ourselves, Paperboy looked at me and asked, "You ready?"

"Fo' sho', cuddy!"

Fidae told me not to just pop mine. She said, "Try chewing it, Dre..." So I stuck to the script I was given and found out how nasty them mothafuckaz really was. I must've made a funny face 'cause when I tasted how sick it was, the homey started busting out laughing.

"What-da-fuck was that?" he asked. "You look mainy!"

"That shit nasty-as-fuck!"

"Here, nigga, wash it down with this liquor!"

He gave me a coffee mug filled with lightning and I swigged that bitch! It took a few seconds before the X hit me. When it did, it immediately gave me a feeling I never felt before. I felt it through my whole body. Then it settled in my brain. The best way I can explain it is that it felt like little bubbles fizzling in my brain!

I must've been drunk and slurring my words a little 'cause I told Paperboy, "Cuddy, my brain thizzin'!"

"What-chu mean? Like bubbly? I feel that shit too!"

"Yeah, Cuddy. This shit thizzin' my brain, P!"

At first, he didn't say anything. It looked like he was thinking something over. Then he said, "Dre, you right! This is Thizz, my nigga!"

From that point on, we didn't call it X no more. It was *Thizz*. We turnt that bitch up that night! I was free-styling non-stop all muthafuckin' night!

The next morning was mainy too! I worked in the kitchen during dinner shift. But, earlier that week they changed my hours to the morning shift. I wasn't used to getting up at 3:30 in the morning to go to work. Especially not after I just spent the whole night thizzin' for the first time.

CHAPTER TWENTY-THREE

"They busted through the door like a locomotive!"
-Mac Dre

I always woke up early on visiting days. Probably around six a.m. so I could make it out there with a clear head by nine. Fidae had left around one in the afternoon. We started partying about two hours later and didn't pass out 'til around three that morning.

It was around 4:20 in the a.m. when the C.O. came to my door talking 'bout, "Get up, Hicks! This door has buzzed three times already! It's work detail."

"I ain't going, I told him."

"Hicks, this is a work call! Are you going to work or not?"

"Man! Suck my dick, honkey! Get the fuck away from my door!"

Now, before I proceed with the rest of this recap I gotta say this: By that time in my term I already knew better than to deliberately pick a fight with the police. Don't get me twisted, if the pigs wanted smoke I'd bring it. But, I learned to stay out

they mothafucking way so I could have my way.

My reaction that morning was pure reflex. First of all, I heard McGraw's voice in that honky when he woke me up. I didn't like that shit.

Anyways, after the pig left, I got up and took a piss. Paperboy was knocked out. Bruh, didn't even stir after I flushed that loud-ass toilet either. I went back to sleep after that.

Can't tell you how long I slept, but I woke up again a little while later. There was noise coming from the other side of the tier. It sounded like a stomping sound. As if a group of people were goose stepping in cadence. I didn't realize it right then and there because I was still hella tired. But I quickly found out what it was. It was the Goon Squad stomping towards my cell in a synchronized march.

Still, even though I heard the stomping, my brain didn't register the notion that they were on their way towards me. It wasn't until a K9 booted my cell door and bellowed, "Andre Hicks, AI4548! Stand up! Face the back wall! Kneel down! Interlock your fingers!"

"Wha-da-fuck!" exclaimed Paperboy.

We both hopped out of bed at the same time. There were ten officers dressed in all black riot gear.

"This is a direct order! Step to the back of the cell-"

"What's up with this shit?!" yelled Paperboy. The K9's didn't reply.

"They came through earlier talking 'bout *work call* and I told 'em to suck my dick!"

"THIS IS LAST AND FINAL WARNING!"

I looked at the homey. The cuddy looked at me. We both looked at the desk where the rest of the pills were.

Paperboy then picked up the last three thizz pills, split 'em with me then turned towards the door and yelled, "Run it, honky! Y'all want it, bring it!"

It seemed like that's all they wanted to hear. That door was immediately snatched open! They busted through it like a locomotive!

They had on helmets face shields, riot gear and padding. The first guy came in with a big plastic shield. Me and the homey

went dumb on they ass. I punched one in the head, but I was hitting a helmet. Paperboy kicked a different one just to get knocked down by the one with the shield a few seconds later.

Within moments, there were so many people in that cage that it got hard for any of us to move. They crashed into that bitch with that shield, bulldozing us into the back wall.

Punches were exchanged. Kicks were booted. Grunts and moans were heard. Ribs were bruised and lips were busted in the process. When it was all said and done, me and Paperboy got whooped then thrown into solitary confinement...

CHAPTER
TWENTY-FOUR

"The Mac had a way of catching you when you were the highest you could be. Then he'd hit you with some cold game so it'll sink in."
-Mac Dre

Anytime you go to the hole you're gonna get overdosed with self-reflection time. It's time when all you got is you. If you've got demons, they're guaranteed to come out in legions...

My first few days were spent sleeping. My head was killing me by day 2. It was a migraine out of this world. I believe it was a withdrawal from not having access to the drinks and drugs I was ingesting while in population. I'm telling you, I was lit as high as could be as often as could be when I was on the yard.

The next few days were given to my animalistic urges. I treated myself with self-inflicted sexual gratification. Then, after that energy was depleted I was left with a feeling of depression. See, without the distraction of music, phone calls, visits or any basic freedoms they gave us I found myself alone with only my thoughts to keep me company. I started tripping off all the shit I was missing.

The one thing that kept me sane those first few days was the mail. Regardless of where you're at, you always get mail. I stayed getting magazines like Source and Vibe.

Every time I saw Bay Area rappers getting their shine on in those magazines I lit up. Even 40 Water was doing his shit! Reppin' for Vallejo as mandated. I didn't give a fuck about him being from the opp side, but I was feeling some type of way as I saw him getting famous because I knew it was supposed to be me reppin' the V on that scale. In my heart I knew if I wouldn't have gone to prison I would've made it big too.

As the days in the hole crept by as slow as a snail going uphill I started reminiscing about the Crest. Me and the cuddies had really did our shit. Together we touched that 'mill ticket and most of it was reinvested into the music industry. The Mac taught us that.

I'll never forget the homey. Bruh, was a real one. They fucked around and took a real nigga when they killed the cuddy. It was a trip 'cause when we was young he had a certain mindset that was ahead of our time. I remember him thuggin' like the rest of us. Stealing cars, breaking into houses and selling singles on the block. But then he went away for a summer. He left with some OG's. None of us ever really knew where he went exactly. But when he came back he came back a real P.I.M.P.!

One time he was sitting in his 'Lac at the Crest Park. We was smoking and he was listening to one of my demo's. We was bobbing our heads to the beat and he really started lacing me up with some elevated game.

"Say, Dre. Let me pull ya' coattail to some of these wise-words."

I smiled because I knew he'd come with some heat. The Mac had a way of catching you when you were the highest you could be. Then he'd hit you with some cold game so it would sink in. He always said weed made you dissect your thoughts.

"You got skills, cuddy. You a true Master At Communicating."

"That's why we Mac's, cuddy," I replied.

"True! As we should be. But check it. Dre, we grew up in the ghetto. Everything around us was on a kill or be killed tip. Whether it's knocking a bitch, or running up to a car with a handful of rocks, we did it with passion."

"That's that 3 C's down shit."

"That's right! That Romper Room shit is what I'm talking 'bout. What we do when that Double R steps on the scene?"

"We go stupid! Niggaz getting money, fucking on bitches. All da' shit."

"Do we give a fuck whose bitch it is?"

"Nope!"

"We loud as fuck too, ain't we?"

"Damn right!"

"The cuddies is wild, Dre. And them bitches love the 'ism. Let's keep it real, don't them off brand niggaz wanna be us too?"

"Yeah. But they imposters."

"True, but check it, cuddy. This music shit is a way for us to share our glow with the rest of the world. Not just the Bay. The whole Bay is like us so of course they gonna embrace us. But this is our way to impact the world! That gangsta' shit is only gonna take us so far. Yeah, you got

Cool Nut, Spice 1 and them niggaz outta Compton... NWA. They capitalizing off that gangsta shit. That's cool, but we got something different. We specialize in fucking bitches, Dre. My truth is entwined in these bitches. Women is where the money's at. The holes they got in they face, they ass, and between they legs is literally gold mines. That's where I get mines. And that's why I rap about this 'ism."

"As you should. I'm not with the fake shit. That's why I rap about real shit too."

"That's what's up. But you also need to see this shit for what it is. Music is a business, Dre. So, if it's a business and you have a product to sell, you need to identify your main consumers. So tell me this: When you get on stage, what do you see?"

"I see fans cheering and having fun."

"Having fun... That's the key, Dre. See, when the cuddies put on them ski masks they not doing that for fun. They doing it for survival. But, fun is the ultimate goal, ain't it? We gotta get that money any which way possible in order to be comfortable enough to kick our feet up and enjoy the finer things in life. The thing is, when niggaz is out there on the weekends, fucking on bitches, they wanna be out of their minds, having stupid fun. Niggaz ain't trying to think 'bout the bullshit they had to do to get there. They just wanna have fun!"

That conversation was imbedded in my mind ever since that day. He didn't just leave it like that, either. He did some shit that afternoon that underlined his words. We picked up some females and took 'em to Sawyer Street where the cuddies be at. Then he made the block rumble. He played different types of music that day. First he played some gangsta shit. Then he played some player shit. He didn't have to explain what he was trying to show me because we were both on the same page. The gangsta shit had the Cuddies on one. The beat did it to us. Plus, the louies were hyenas so we were always ready to get into some shit. But when he played that smooth shit, the breezies turnt' up which in turn got the cuddies on they player shit.

I got the point he was making. But, on an artistic level I don't think I was ready to embrace the ultimate message. Being in solitary confinement made me think about all that shit. I was still thinking about how the thizz had my brain fizzing. It was the best high I ever felt. While mulling all that over in my head at the same time I had an epiphany. I decided I needed to make music that accentuated that high. Something niggaz could go stupid to. I wanted to make music that would make niggaz hyper. But at the same time, I wanted to keep it gutta. I had to keep shit fly. That's how I came up with the word *hyphy*. It's a mixture of the words hyper and fly. It describes the energy that my music is 'posed to bring out in niggaz when they listen to it.

Hyphy!

They kept me in the hole for 90 days before they released me back to into population. That shit was hard, but I was thankful for the solitude 'cause it gave me the time to really cultivate a plan.

Something else took place when I was in solitary that kinda changed my life. One day, at mail call the C.O. walked by and slid an envelope under the door. When I picked it up, I didn't recognize the handwriting and the return address said Sacramento. I had no idea who it was from.

When I opened the envelope a picture fell out of a blonde haired white girl. She looked familiar but I couldn't be sure. I had been getting fan mail a lot during the beginning of my term. It could've been anyone so I read the letter:

Dear Dre,

I don't know if you'll remember me. We met one night a few years back when you did a show at the Courtyard.

I'm writing because I saw your case in the Vallejo Times and I knew you were in prison. It took me a while to reach out to you. And even a longer time to find you.

That night we spent together will forever be etched in my mind. I never experienced anything like that before. I just wanted you to know that. If you ever want to talk about anything. If you ever need anything, please contact me.

This is my address and my phone number is at the top of this page. I'm curious as to how you're holding up in there and I would very much like to hear from you.

Sincerely yours,

Noel Ellis

I don't know what it was, but after reading that letter I knew that snow bunny was gonna end up being my bottom bitch. I didn't really know her, but I remembered the feeling she left me with that night. It was a classy, wealthy and smooth vibe.

Something I've learned over the years is with everything life throws at you, you're not gonna remember everything. Especially when you got fast talking individuals stepping to you with game. You might not even remember a person's face or name. When you're outta your body from the drinks and the drugs. You won't always download what you see or hear.

But there's one thing you won't ever forget. It's how a mothafucka makes you feel... You'll always remember how a person made you feel. So once I realized who this lady was, I knew she was my key to another level of living.

I called baby the same day I got out the hole and every day after that until I came home!

We built a relationship. She wrote me, answered my collect calls and sent me money for store.

I ended up finding out that ol' girl had married an older white guy who was banker from Sacramento. He had big money. Him talking 'bout old money! They weren't together two years before he died and left her with everything. She was breaded up and didn't have to worry about shit. Not only was she financially stable, she came with A-1 credit too.

I've never been known to squander an opportunity. Especially the ones that only come around once in a lifetime. I got into her head with this Crestside 'ism and she was locked in for life!

CHAPTER TWENTY-FIVE

*"It's really an extension of the game and the
Mob controls who gets in, stays on, or is taken out."*
-Mac Dre

I got out of the Feds in 1996. It was poppin'! All kinds of shit was in play that summer. The East Coast - West Coast feud was in full effect. I stayed in my lane though. I met Pac a few times before I went in. The nigga was a beast, but I missed the wave he was on.

I had just got out and was trying to get my shit together. The Bay was going through a drought when it came to nationwide attention. If you weren't from L.A. or N.Y. your music wasn't really getting any play. It wasn't that the Bay didn't have good music, we just didn't have the spotlight at the time.

As soon as I stepped out, I went straight back to the ghetto. Vallejo was my home and the Crest was where I held the thrown. I came home and immediately met up with the cuddies. Mac Mall and Coolio were doing their shit. Pounding the pavement with their 'ism.

I had so many plans in my head, I hit the ground running. I came home and stepped straight into my own house and a Black on Black Beemer. From the outside looking in, a nigga came home ballin'. But, in my mind, I wasn't nowhere near where I needed to be. I knew how to get there though.

I was dead set on bringing the hyphy movement into play. The turf already had a gang of young niggaz that was 'bout that energy, so the timing was perfect. The Bay was already hyphy.

In a perfect world, I would've gotten straight out to a nationwide tour along with a big-boy record deal with an established record company. But that wasn't my reality. I came home to a few obstacles and two of them was McGraw and his sidekick, Nichelman. They were on some bitch shit from the gate.

I had six months of probation to do for the Feds when I hit the bricks. I'll never forget that first day out. I got out on a Thursday so I had to check in to the local Police Department before the weekend started. I showed up at the VPD at 6 a.m. But look how they did me. Them mothafuckaz had me sitting in the lobby 'til 5 p.m. on some straight bullshit!

They had to photograph me and take my fingerprints. And the games didn't stop their. Them bitches left me in a holding cell for three hours after that. Then, a little after eight, McGraw and Nichelman both came in on some bullshit. When I saw McGraw I was actually taken aback. The years hadn't been good to the honky. He had a bald head and a beer belly.

"So, Mac Dre," he started. "They finally let you, huh?"

"That's obvious. The real question is why y'all had me in this bitch so mothafuckin' long."

"You're lucky I don't take you in right now. We got a cell for you at the county jail with your name on it. There's a few unsolved robberies I'm sure we can pin on your dumb ass if we wanted to."

"Man, fuck you! You gonna let me out or what? If I would've known you bitches was gonna come with this bullshit I would've came with my lawyer."

Then Nichelman's nickel and dime ass spoke up, "Your lawyers didn't seem to be much of a help on getting you out of doing all that time, Dre. What makes you think they can help you now?"

I knew they was on some real life nonsense so I decided not to feed into their ruse. I was hot, though. So I bit down on my jaw and held my tongue.

"What? You ain't got nothing to say, Mr. Motor Mouth. Mr. Fuck the VPD?"

They ended up letting me out that night, but that was the beginning of a continuous 'bout with the police department. They were dead serious about harassing ya' boy. They followed me everywhere. Had cop cars parked in front of my house 24 hours a day!

It didn't matter though. I was on a mission to crack the code to the music industry and nothing was gonna stop that. What I didn't realize at the time was the music game is a lot like the game. It's really an extension of the game and the Mob controls who gets in, stays on, or is taken out.

Yeah, I said *Mob*. There's Mob ties in every major city where mainstream music is coming out of.

In L.A. Death Row was running shit. Suge Knight was having shit knocked down and nobody could get into the industry without his clearance. At least, that's how things were when I first got out the Feds.

When Suge and Puffy went to war, niggaz was getting killed left and right. If you weren't really connected in the underworld circles you would've just thought Diddy was square, but the nigga's a killa. He had a million dollar bounty on Suge and Pac's head.

Later on, after Death Row and Bad Boy slowed their roll, Master P and his No Limit Soldiers took the game's reins. I knew Master P from the Bay. The nigga was a Richmond nigga, but he got muscled out by the Mob and ended up get sent back to the South. That's part of the game the public wasn't privy to.

After P, Baby and Slim took over. Y'all know them niggaz came up off dog food. Them niggaz had real drug money. They bought their way in but they still had to shed blood because Master P didn't give up his spot that easily. I'm telling you, shit was happening behind the scenes that most people don't even know about.

Even though I was in the music industry before I got locked up, I didn't know about the organized crime element of it all. Yeah, I know a lot of rappers were thuggin'. But I didn't know shit was organized like that. I wasn't a Made Man when I got locked up. But 40 was. That's how he had all that work when we were younger. I had no idea at the time. Eventually, it all came out though.

I was free. That's what trumped all the obstacles that were thrown my way. Shit didn't come as easy as I thought it would. Nevertheless, I was out. I got to hug my momma. Smoke and drink with the louies and beat the shit outta some pussy! I was in a good position any which way you looked at it.

Can't forget the snow bunny. Baby showed up at my momma's house about a week after I got out in an all white Lexus LI. That bitch (the car) was so clean, I didn't invite her inside. I got in her shit right there on the curb. The air was blowing and she had a blunt already rolled for a nigga.

The VPD was up the street taking pictures of everything. I'm sure they ran baby's plates but I also knew she was cleaner than a whistle. They was annoying, but what could you do? Fuck 'em... That was my mentality.

Baby wasn't feelin' it at all. First thing out her mouth was, "What's up with that?"

"They stay harassing a nigga. I told you they was on some bullshit in my city. They been parked out there since the day I got out. No joke."

"Dude, you must've pissed someone off in a major way."

I laughed 'cause she was square-as-fuck. But, then again she wasn't.

"Dre, I wanna fuck right now!"

"Is that right?"

"I've been waiting way too long. And, it's kinda turning me on that they're out there watching us."

"What you sayin'?" I asked, taking a closer look at her pretty-ass.

"You wanna give 'em a show?"

"Naw, ma," I laughed. "We can't do all that. They'll hall us in for indecent exposure."

"Damn. Okay. Let's go."

"Where?"

"How 'bout we start from the beginning? Where we first met."

I thought about it for a moment, knowing where she was talking about. Then I told her to drive. Baby was raw. I had already hit a few bitches over the weekend, but I was ready for her. I'd been plotting on killing that cat for a few years already. Plus, in my eyes, she paid her choosing fee by fucking with a nigga while I was down.

Then, just when I thought she was gonna turn the car on and pull away from the curb she looked at me and said, "Lean your seat back. Fuck them pigs! These windows got limo tint on them. They can't see in here and I've been waiting too long. I'm not gonna wait another second!"

The bitch knew how to turn it up when she wanted to. I shrugged my shoulders then leaned that mothafuckin' seat back. The second she pulled the anaconda out I saw her eyes widen like she hadn't seen it before. I remember her telling me she hadn't fucked with a nigga as big as me before and by the way she was looking at it I could tell she still hadn't fucked with a swipe as long as mine. Her eyes couldn't lie.

With no hesitation, she opened up wide and took me in her mouth. She sucked the fuck outta the head. It filled her mouth as it grew. Then she started going in deeper and deeper as she made it wet with her spit. She almost got half of it in by the time she pulled back. I wasn't going for all that. I grabbed the back of her head and pushed her back down on it.

Baby didn't stutter. She went all in.

Committed to that sin wholeheartedly; she sped up. Going faster and faster; deeper and deeper every time she came down.

Baby was working it. My shit was hard as fuck! I felt it hitting the back of her throat every time she went down on it. Her tongue was going crazy with it. Licking on my shit, squeezing the head and all. Her head game was tremendous!

That shit felt so good I almost couldn't control myself. I wrapped my hand in her hair and started pushing her down harder and deeper. She was slurping and sucking on me so hard I felt my balls constrict like they was ready to bust.

Then I felt the inside of her throat. I was in there. At first, it was like my head had found another hole. She gagged too. But I went in harder and half the head went in. She gagged again. Then, bam! I pushed in so hard I felt it slide into her throat. Fuck! That shit felt hella good!

She wasn't with the complaining shit either. She bounced her head on my shit like a jackhammer. Making my shit disappear every fucking time she went down on it! I had never, ever met a bitch in my life who could swallow my whole dick like that. Her nose was pressing against my groin. She was steady chocking, but she kept going! That throat was tighter, wetter and warmer than any pussy I ever had in my life!

"Damn!" I moaned. "I'm 'bout to bust, bitch! You ready for this?"

She changed gears when I said all that. She pulled off my shit, my whole dick was wet-as-fuck, dripping saliva. Then she put the head back in her mouth and went to work on that. She started dropping down real fast on the head while stroking the base with her right hand.

"Fuuuck!" I yelled.

I busted a fat-ass nut in her mouth. Noel swallowed every drop of it too! I was twitching! Ya' boy's fuck face was on some ugly shit! By the time baby pulled my shit out her mouth I was hooked.

That's when I really decided she was gonna be the wifey...

CHAPTER TWENTY-SIX

"What's your definition of loyalty?"
-Noel Ellis

The sound of music changed while I was away. But, the industry hadn't. The labels who were well connected had control over their region. You might not understand how deep that statement is, but you will once you keep reading.

Another aspect of the game that didn't change was how you came up in it. You had to have money to get established in 1996 and '97. It was right before niggaz could go viral off an Instagram video. You still had to build your following through traditional routes like word of mouth. Becoming a multiplatinum selling artist has always been harder than getting an NBA contract.

The cuddies were waiting with open arms when I came home. Coolio and Mall were the only Romper Room cuddies who didn't get indicted by the State or the Feds. They were the main niggaz I was fucking with when I touched down. When they sat me down to chop game we talked about the music industry and the game as if it were one in the same. We knew exactly what needed to be done in order for us to make it, too. Problem was, coming up with the proper amount of start up capital.

I'ma tell you right now, Mac Dre doesn't move backwards. If a cuddy crosses me, I'm done with him. If a bitch crosses me, I'm done with her. If I have to struggle to get into a room through the front door, I'll find a window. That's how I think. It's always been like that with me. So, when the cuddies agreed to get organized in order to climb our way up the totem pole, I agreed. However, there was no way in hell I was gonna step back into the car with the ski mask alumni. We needed huge sums of money, but not that way. I had a whole 'nother way to do it this time around.

Thizz was my drug of choice ever since the first time I tried it. Every time I popped a pill I went dumb on the mic. When I told the cuddies 'bout it, they said it was nothing for them to get it. Thizz was in the Bay in a major way! They had a plug with some Asians who had boats for twenty-five hundred.

A boat is a thousand pills. That was a cool-ass price at the time. It gave us leeway to get really paid. The only problem was I was on Federal probation. Them alphabet boys had they eyes on me and I wasn't trying to be a statistic raising the recidivism rate.

The fact that I was on a Federal leash couldn't be ignored. Yet, it couldn't be allowed to stop or slow down the movement either. So we moved forward.

Then, something took place that changed the playing field in our favor. It was a situation that ended up mixing the California Valley's gang culture with the Bay Area's pimp/player/hustler culture.

No one, not even myself would've ever guessed how much of an affect a conversation that took place in between the sheets at the Marriot would've had on the whole Northern California street culture.

After Noel sucked the kids out my nuts in her Lexus we went back to the spot where we met. She somehow managed to rent the same room we spent that winter night together. We was up late into the night that night. Not just fucking, but talking. Talking about all kinds of shit. I'll never forget when she told me... "Dre, I know you have a lot going for you. You're a genius at what you do. You're the chosen one and nothing is going to stop you from reaching the heights you are meant to reach. You can do, and will do it with or without me. But, I also know I can help you if you let me. I can change your life right now... Right now, Dre."

I didn't say anything. Instead, I looked into the windows of her soul and studied her authenticity. After seeing nothing but sincerity I asked, "What'chu mean you can change my life?"

"I can give you something you've never had."

"What's that?"

"Stability. I have a four bedroom house with a pool in the back. That comes with all my money and my credit, which is A-1, by the way. I can give you a safe and comfortable place to rest your head when you come home from the streets."

I didn't let it show on my face, but I was feelin' every word she was spitting. Living with her was always in the plan. I was just taking my time with it.

"I hear you," I said. "You gotta understand some shit, though. I'm a rapper. My career is gonna keep me on the road for weeks at a time. There's gonna be situations where-"

"I know what I'm getting myself into and I fully understand the assignment, Dre. I know what comes with being with a celebrity. All I ask is you don't bring any diseases home. Keep the streets in the streets. Keep our home safe and don't bring any other woman in my face."

Now, it was her turn to read my thoughts. My emotionless mask wasn't easily decipherable, but she was a woman. Women have an extra strong sense of intuition. I'm sure she knew my heart's truth.

Then she continued, "If you give me an answer right now I'll buy you a Range Rover this weekend."

On God, I was doing backflips when I heard that. But all she saw was this Country Club Crest face.

"A Range ain't shit without your word," I told her while holding her stare.

"What!?"

"I demand loyalty. I get what you're asking of me and I respect it. But you need to overstand my expectations too. I need pure, unadulterated loyalty."

"What's your definition of loyalty?"

"First of all, rep me when I'm not around."

"Already do."

"Be a lady in the streets."

"I don't know how to be anything else."

"A freak in the bed."

"Is that aspect in question?"

"There's more... Never speak on my business. Not to your friends, family, the police or a priest! If I ask you for something - anything - don't question me. Take the loss right then and there. If you can deliver all these things, I'll give you my word that I'll give you what you want in exchange."

Baby smiled, leaned forward and gave me a kiss. Then she said, "I can do all that and more."

When the weekend showed up we took a trip to the car lot. Baby co-signed for me and I got an all white on white Range Rover. That bitch was raw! The Chrome rims were so shiny they blinded mothatfuckaz who stared too long. Not only did she put that pretty mothafucka in my name, she did some player shit the second the papers were signed. She told me to do me for the rest of the weekend. She didn't even wanna stunt with a nigga that weekend. Noel knew I was gonna floss with the louies on some turf shit so she gave me space.

It was on! I went straight to the Crest, swooped up Coolio and Mall. We went to King's Market on some hyphy shit in a real way.

Before long, the parking lot looked like a car show. The cuddies came through in everything from Blazers to Benzes and Beemers! The daytime sideshow was in full effect! Music was pounding the pavement. Burnt rubber filled the air. Bitches was out showing all their assets. And the cuddies were flossing to the best of they capabilities.

We had been out there for a minute. Liquor was flowing. Trees were floating. Thizz was chewed. It was a beautiful day in the ghetto. Then someone yelled, "Let's go to Oakland!"

That really made us hyphy. Everyone started hopping into their rides ready to pull out when suddenly, the vibe got ruined. Vallejo PD came in from everywhere! McGraw led a battalion straight into our cypher. They looked as hostile as the Clan could ever look.

I'm not gonna say the coppers never came into the Crest terrorizing shit. They have. But, there's times when the right people are out and about and niggaz is ready to push back. On that day, we outnumbered the pigs three to one. There were homegirls, OG's, cuddies of all ages, plus civilians in attendance and we were all having a good time. Mothafuckaz wasn't trying to hear what them crackers had to say.

I'm sure by the way them folks rushed on the scene that everyone out there had a moment where they felt that flight or fight sense kick in. And I can speak for the group when I say we all chose to fight. The cuddies all grouped up and faced the pigs ready to press play on 'em.

"Whose car is this?" asked McGraw after he hopped out his unmarked Crown Vic.

He was talking about the Range. I shook my head knowing he already knew the answer to that question.

"Hmmm... Let me guess," he started. "This must be Dre's car." After scoffing at the opulence of my whip he turned towards one of his minions and barked, "Tow this shit! Ms. Ellis can go get it from the tow yard herself."

"Bitch-ass honky! This my shit!" I yelled when I heard him giving them directions to tow my Rover.

One thing I can say about McGraw is that he's a bold bitch. The thugs were in war mode. The rollers were outnumbered, and he still didn't give a fuck. He walked straight up to me, putting his stank-ass nose way to close to mines.

It was one of the hardest tests of my life. I had to reach real deep to find the power not to slap his bitch-ass! The louies would've rocked too!

All it would've took was for me to swing and shit would've went up like the Fourth of July!

He must've sensed the mood of the day because he ended up yielding. After a helluva staring contest took place he took a step back.

"Just so you know," McGraw started. "I'm pulling this car over every time it's in traffic. All my men have instructions to do so as well. Since you're on Federal probation we can tear this motherfucker up in ways that'll break your heart, Dre."

"Get out my face, bitch!"

"Ha!" he laughed then turned to another officer. "You guys hear this felon?" Then he turned back to me and scoffed, "I'm going to stay in your face, Mac Dre! That, I can promise you!"

He stepped away just as I reached my limit of self restraint. That pig bounced but his goons stayed. The tow truck came so fast it had to have been planned. It was as if the driver had been parked around the corner just waiting for McGraw's call.

The whole turf saw the harassment and started tripping. The rollers had to protect the tow truck driver 'cause niggaz was acting up. Throwing cups and all kinds of trash at the mothafucka.

That was a wake up call. I knew I had to leave. A lot of people talk shit about rappers who leave the hood when they get rich and famous. What they don't realize is once you hit a certain level of the game, you become a target. Not only do the hyenas start salivating but the cops do too. I never received flak for leaving 'cause the cuddies saw the circumstances I was faced with. But I've seen other artists go through all kinds of internal conflicts in their neighborhood for leaving. Niggaz get smutted up because most people don't understand what comes with becoming a big fish in a small pond.

When I called to tell Noel what happed, I didn't just hit her with the bullshit of the day. I had to discuss something way more important than getting the Range back. The second she picked up her phone the first words out my mouth were, "Come get me so I can move all my shit to our house..."

CHAPTER TWENTY-SEVEN

"My plan was to be independent. That wasn't going to happen if I entered the game in the red."
-Mac Dre

Noel's house quickly became my house. But, on paper, I lived at my momma's house. Moms' was cool with it and the cuddies understood too. Especially since ever since I came home, the pigs had the turf smelling like a BLT.

I was residing in Sacramento by my third week out. I ain't gonna lie, my house was clean! It was a two story house. The upstairs had three bedrooms and two full baths! One of the rooms was Noel's office. Baby worked at the State Capital. The extra room had two beds in it for guests.

The Master bedroom was my favorite room in the house. Big screen TV; a little kitchen with the microwave and mini fridge. A walk in closet. Two showers and a his and hers sink. The master bedroom also had a patio overlooking the backyard, and there was a spa out there. I spent many nights soaking with a blunt in my mouth.

Downstairs had a den, dining room, extra bedroom and another bathroom. The living room and kitchen was big-as-fuck too! Everything in the house was new and top of the line.

In the backyard there was a deck with a manmade waterfall and stream. There was also an elevated garden making the yard a small maze! You could actually get lost in that bitch if you took the wrong turns. In the center of it there was a table where a nigga could have private conversations over some brunch. Real player shit.

Every real go-getter needs a honeycomb hideout. It doesn't gotta be all opulent and shit. But it should be clean and peaceful. Your home life can mean the difference between a calm mind or a hot head. If your home life isn't on point, it could knock you off your square.

You should have the same thought process when choosing your main bitch. When you come home to her she's supposed to give you peace, help you calm your nerves. If you got a messy bitch at home you'll never have time to recharge. You'll never have a clear head. A good woman will give you peace and that's important when you're in the streets.

Sometimes, it's not all about being with a specific person either. It can be an energy that comes from your environment. It's like your house, your room, even your prison cell can represent the inner sanctions of your mind. If your room, house or office is cluttered then chances are, your mind is cluttered too.

That's why that spot was so important to my productive side. Some people think you can't upgrade and move out the ghetto or you'll lose your edge. That shit ain't true. A nigga like me can't lose his edge 'cause I stay in the trenches. Nevertheless, I appreciated a clean and safe environment. And that's exactly what Noel gave me.

After getting my living arrangements together the next step was getting into the studio. That part of the plan wasn't a problem at all. There were a few different studios I could go to. The problem with that was I was gonna have to go to one of my industry connects to front me some studio time. I didn't wanna do that 'cause I didn't wanna owe anybody shit. I'm not blind to the fact that anytime you use someone else's resources it puts you in a position where you're indebted to them. My ultimate plan was to go independent. That wasn't going to happen if I entered the game in the red. The music industry is the last hustle where you wanna owe anybody anything.

I remember having a conversation with Too Short where he told me if he would've only negotiated one or two more dollars per album he sold back in the 80's and early 90's he would've been rich enough to really retire. He would've retired after his third album. I never forgot that, and that's what motivated me to go independent.

My goal was to put my own studio together. Start my own company. I already knew what I'd call it and how I was gonna put the money together to make it happen. I was gonna call it THIZZ ENT and I was going to fund it by selling Thizz!

When I got out of prison the Bay Area had an established music industry. We were definitely on the map, but not like the major labels were. We didn't have the mainstream's ear. The only way I was gonna be able to crack that glass ceiling was by getting a whole region behind me. A whole metropolitan area behind me.

I had Vallejo backing me. That came with the rest of the Bay Area, but the Bay was saturated with rappers. Sacramento wasn't.

Sacramento wasn't really popping like that in the rap game. So I decided to play chess. I set out to make a name for myself in Sac and the surrounding areas.

I did that by pushing thizz. Me and the cuddies started going to every club, sports bar, motorcycle club; every function, house party and cookout we could get into. It was like we were politicking. All the while, I'm turning it up at all the parties. It was a win-win scenario. I promoted my music while the louies pushed the thizz.

We didn't stop at the functions, either. We brought that sideshow culture to the Valley. The clubs close at two a.m. And niggaz ain't always ready to call it a night. What we did was make sure every party we attended had an after party. That was easy since Sideshows can take place wherever you ready to turn up at.

In the Bay Area, sideshows had been popping for years. A sideshow could be anywhere as long as you had space to do Donuts in a hot whip; pop wheelies on ya' motorbike and beat up the block with them speakers in the trunk of your car!

We the reason Cali niggaz installed foot railings on their scrapers. We had niggaz ghost riding whips. It was nothing to see a car with tremendous beat riding by driverless with like four of five cuddies on its hood, trunk or roof! We called it going Dumb!

The Valley, especially Sacramento had a strong gang culture. bloods and crips controlled the streets and the vibes that came out of them. That didn't stop us though. We had crips and bloods at the same sideshow thizzin' to Romper Room music. After a while, we just followed the parties. It wasn't just Sac where we did this. We were everywhere. We went to Stockton, Fresno, Bakersfield, San Jose, Vallejo, Richmond, Oakland, EPA, Pittsburgh an Frisco!

Shit got popping for real! Then one day I got a call that changed everything.

It was about a year after I got out. I was at the house making plans for a welcome home party for the cuddies . J Diggs and Curt were coming home that weekend. I usually didn't answer calls from numbers I didn't recognize but something told me to answer this certain call that came out the blue.

I really didn't think about it when I answered it, "Yeah... who 'dis?"

"Dre. This C-Bo. I got your number from Mall."

I met C-Bo before I got locked up but I never really vibed with him. Not for any particular reason. We just didn't have a reason to fuck with it. By the time I got out the Feds Bo had hooked up with Pac and them Death Row niggaz so he was definitely pushing units. I had to respect it. Either way, his call came unexpected.

"Yeah," I told him. "It's good. What's up wit' it?"

"I gotta holla at you in person. I'm in town right now. Can we meet up?"

"Where you at?"

"I'm in the Heights."

"Shit, Arden mall is right around the corner. I can be there whenever."

"On crip, that's what's up! What about we hook up at the food court in thirty minutes?"

"Done!"

"A'ight."

I wasn't busy and the mall was literally right up the street from where I lived. I Didn't even have to get dressed 'cause I stayed fitted from the moment I woke up. So I hopped in the Rover and headed over there.

C-Bo isn't hard to spot in a crowd. He stays with a bald head, he's kinda stocky too. That day, I pushed up on him he was wearing blue Chucks Taylors, some grey Levi's with a deep crease down the front. With a blue and black checkered button up. A real 29th Street crip! I had to respect it especially since Sacramento had mostly bloods running the trenches.

I found Bo at a table in the food court. When I approached him he stood up and gave me dap then said, "I ordered us some Chinese food. I'm hungry than a bitch! I don't know what you fuck with so I ordered a little bit of everything."

There were ribs, fried chicken, shrimp fried rice and some egg rolls. I was a thousand percent wit' those activities. I immediately took a seat! The conversation took place while we ate and didn't take too long too get started.

Bo started it by saying, "I called you 'cause I wanna holla at you 'bout something classified. You're about to hear some serious shit. But I know you're a real nigga so I trust what I tell you is gonna benefit both of us."

"Okay," I said between a mouthful of fried rice.

"Dre, your name's been ringing so I-"

"Ringing? What 'dat mean? Somebody got a problem?"

"Naw. You shinin', cuz."

"So, what's good? You tryna do a compilation? I know what you doing with Mob Figgaz is heat."

"Yeah, we killin' the game. But Thizz Ent is doing some shit too."

"It is, we doing our shit."

"As you should... Dre, I'ma get to the point. Before you went to the Feds you and your niggaz were doing big thangs. I tip my hat to your set. Then, when y'all fell, no one fell with you. I know how this game is and there's no way the Feds didn't step to you on some snitch shit based on what you was doing in the industry. On top of that, your hood really fucks with you so I know you're official."

"I'm a real affiliate."

"Niggaz been waiting for you to get out. We been sitting back, watching how you move."

"I'm doing me!"

"That's right. We see that. You got something nice going with the X too."

When he said that last statement his whole demeanor seemed to change. Suddenly I sensed a little animosity. I could tell his message was a double entendre. We both knew it. I saw the quick icy glare so it snapped me into war mode. I wasn't sure where he was going with his train of thought. Shit, Sac was his hometown, maybe he had a problem with the louies cornering the ecstasy market. I didn't know. So I waited for him to clarify where he was headed. Either way, I had no problem with knocking his ass out if he got at me sideways.

"And?" I said. "What's up?"

He paused a little while before he continued, "We got a whole movement built by niggaz just like you. Just like me. Hear me out, cuz. The Mob Figgaz isn't just a cool name, Dre. We're a mafia. We control shit. We touch and control most of the guns and drugs that come through Northern California. It ain't nothing new, either. This movement has been in play for decades. The rap game ain't nothing but a front for the dirty money we all been making. I know this can't be a surprise. You know how the game is. I bet you was making way more money hitting banks than you were with the music, right?"

"Maybe."

"But the rap game-"

"Gave a nigga a license-"

"Exactly!" he said.

"Exactly. So, like I was saying. We got a table up here who works together in too many ways to list. We are all bosses in our own right. Niggaz like Fed X, Hussla, AP9, Too Short and 40-"

"40?"

"Yeah! 40 been at the table since way before you went to prison. Dre, what I'm telling you is real! We push and we push hard. Not only do we control the streets, we also control the industry."

"Suge, Diddy and all them niggaz got the industry on lock right now."

"On a commercial level, you're right. But the key words is 'right now.' Them niggaz got major label deals. But that don't mean they not as dirty as us. They just as grimy as we are and they most definitely respect our minds too. There's an underworld that's operating right under people's noses. It's been going since the 80's."

The shit he was telling me was bonkers. I couldn't believe what I was hearing. But, Bo was a real street nigga. He wasn't one to play games like that. At least, that's what I thought of him.

"So, what you saying?" I asked him.

"There's a council and I'm proposing to give you a seat at the table. 40 and Jacka already co-signed for you too."

"40?"

"Yeah. Why you so surprised? Y'all from the same city. Cuz got a lot of respect for you. You could've snitched on a lot of people when you fell but you didn't and niggaz know this. Dre, the thizz you movin' ain't shit. We can make it where you and your niggaz is pushing boats instead of party packs. If that's what you wanna do, you got it! 'Cept, as a made man you gonna be pushing shit on cross country tours. You still gonna push with your squad, you'll just be on a larger scale. You'll have to pay extra attention to the snakes too. Shit gets grimy when you hit this next level."

"Thizz nation," I though out loud.

"Exactly."

"So, what's expected of me in return. Nothing in life is free."

"You're expected to be there for the rest of the mob. Control your team. And stay loyal. We all protect and provide for one another. Everything from plugs, weapons, lawyer money, industry connections and more, we're all there for one another. And, Dre... This ain't no music deal. It's mob shit."

"What I gotta do?"

"I wanted to touch base with you first before we bring this to the table. I don't see why you wouldn't clear. Once you do, we'll get at you. We'll meet up and you can meet the fellaz."

"And if I don't clear?"

"You're a real nigga, Dre. I respect ya' gangsta'. But if you don't make the cut, you ain't finna get any bigger that you are right now. You starting to pick up traction, but we control everything that moves across Northern Cali..."

With all that said and done we finished eating and went our separate ways. It took me a minute to digest what he told me. I went home, walked through the maze in the backyard and sat down at the table to smoke me a blunt while I contemplated what had been presented to me. I was glad the cuddies were coming home soon. The timing was perfect. If things went bad and I needed some real niggaz behind me they would be the ones who rode hardest. I knew I could trust them with my life in a life or death situation...

The Mac (R.I.P.) would've led us to the next level if his life wouldn't have ended so soon. So the torch was handed to me to lead the Federation of louies to the upper echelon rooms where the fellaz networked.

Getting drafted by the Mob opened doors to me that otherwise would have stayed sealed shut. What most people don't see or understand about the music industry is that every major city or State has Mob affiliates. If one faction is at odds with another, those groups won't have access to each other's State. This affects people's bottom line since most of our legal revenue comes from doing shows. Back then, before the internet, it could also mean your albums wouldn't be carried in certain regions of the country.

Eighty-five percent of the population doesn't understand the psychology behind most of the commercial sales that are made in this country and around the world. People don't understand that the choices of what they think is bangin' or not is made for them before the music ever makes it to the stores.

It's like this: No one on this earth is truly unique. Most people like to think they aren't sheep but they are. Whether you know it or not, everything you do is a mirrored behavior of what you've seen others do or say around you or in the media. From the hairstyles and clothes you wear to the music you listen to, it's all being dictated for you by the powers that be.

The Mob taught me this. Since the world is populated with pastures full of deaf, dumb and blind sheep, all you gotta do is learn to lead them like a Shepard. You can actually coerce the culture in many different ways. Implanting thoughts through subliminal notions is like planting seeds that sprout whatever kind of money trees you want them to.

If you're driving through your city and see someone sitting at a bus stop rocking a thizz t-shirt then you look up and see my face on a billboard, your mind is gonna start telling you I'm the shit! Once that happens you'll want to experience and associate yourself with the vibe that's associated with my movement.

Some of you might think anyone can buy billboards and print shirts. They can if they got the bread to do it. But that doesn't mean their investments will actually interpret into cash. The streets have to respect you.

When I met Big Meech, cuddy had hella billboards pushing BMF in Atlanta. He did it in Miami too. It worked for him and his movement because he was a certified Mafia Don. It wasn't the music industry that made him a boss it was them twenty-five hundred keys a month he was supplying his region with.

Cash Money was another movement with mafia ties. If you let the media tell it, Cash Money hit the scene with a thirty million dollar deal from an extra large label. Slim did get that deal for them. However, they were only put in that position because of how deep in the game they were. Baby's brother had a hit squad that shot and clawed themselves to the top. They controlled all the tar that flooded their area. You couldn't move in their section without their blessings.

The manipulation can be so subtle you won't even realize when or where it's happening. It's a science that upper echelon niggaz been perfecting for decades.

CHAPTER TWENTY-EIGHT

"When my guys fuck wit' your guys, that's mob ties."
-Mac Dre

Some opportunities only come along once in a lifetime. All the pieces of the puzzle have to line up in order for you to truly capitalize off the breaks I'm talkin' about. The proposition C-Bo came at me with was one of those chances. The fact that my day ones were coming home at the same time was the pieces of the puzzle I'm talking about. Having a full lineup of niggaz who I could truly trust one thousand percent was the universe giving me my just due.

When Diggs and Kilo came home the whole team was once again back together. We all sat down to really chop game on the first night they came home. That was when I not only laced them up on my plan to make Thizz Ent the biggest label in the country, I also laced them up on what Bo had told me. When it was all said and done it came out that Mall and Coolio had heard whispers of music related mafia ties. But they had never been presented with the actual proof of its legitimacy.

In the months to come, I had a chance to chop game with the Mob. It's a trip to me, how much I found out about the careers of rappers who came and went during the 90's. Certain individuals came up, others faded away. A few of the names, you've probably never heard of by design. A few of them lost their lives before their careers had the chance to flourish. What most people didn't understand was that a portion of those lives were taken because mob ties were broken. In other words, they were victims of sanctioned hits.

What I also found out was that me and the louies had been on the Mob's radar long before we caught our prison terms. The Mac was a prospect about to be inducted but he died too soon. Then our push came up for consideration. We didn't make the cut which was fucked up 'cause if we had been drafted into the major leagues none of us would've ever seen the Feds.

The reason we didn't make the cut earlier was because we were too goonish. When we were young, on them ski masked capers, no one could tell us shit. We were so hot we brought the Feds to Vallejo.

Niggaz pushing metric tons push a different way. When they eat, the table only has seats for gangstaz. And in case you don't know, there is a difference between a goon and a gangsta.

A goon doesn't utilize finesse. He takes what he wants by force. He's out of control; hyphy and dangerously loose.

A gangsta plays chess, not checkers. He can focus on his goal and manipulate things in ways that leave his mark with offers that can't be refused.

The key word there is *offers*. Gangstaz never push a person into a corner like a goon would.

The cuddies were certified goonies in the 80's and early 90's. There was no turning us down because we didn't know any other way.

But, let me get back on topic. If you hear, see or read an article from one of your favorite rappers speaking good about another rapper, it's a co-sign. When one artist has a guest appearance on another's album, it's a co-sign. These are all tactics made to lead the sheep into a specified area.

The truth of the matter is the rap game is a large scale front for illegal activities. There's a lot of niggaz out there eating. They're pushing foreign whips, feeding whole cliques. I'll tip my hat to that. But riddle me this: How many of you can pick up a burner phone and order 250k worth of whatever product you push at wholesale prices? How many of y'all can pick up that type of work within 24 hours of putting in that order?

Keep it real...

If I was Marco I wouldn't be hearing too many of y'all calling out 'Polo. The average street nigga just isn't that high up on the totem pole. I wasn't even on that level until I was inducted into the mafia.

The Mob is deeper than a secret society. We all serve a purpose. We all move cohesively. The game is chess-like meaning a wrong move can cost ya' a life. On Romper Room gang, it's real!

My perks kicked in as soon as I became a made man. There are a string of music studios owned by the Mob located all over Northern California. I suddenly had access to every single one of them.

Of course, there's rules and regulations. If you need to use a producer or engineer you need to pay them for their time. There's never fighting or arguing over studio time since first dibs goes to whoever owns the studio. Every faction is expected to build their own studio, too. That wasn't a problem for me since that was part of the plan anyway.

My second major perk was the thizz plug! I loved thizz and the Asians had me on one. But through a Mob connect I had a line straight from the Red Light district in Amsterdam. They had thizz for twenty-five cents a piece! I was getting double and triple stacks for fifty cents and seventy-five cents each! C-Bo was right. Fucking with the Mob put in a position to sell Boats.

Then came the tours! We took that hyphy movement all up and down the West Coast and all throughout the Midwest. In the late 90's the music industry was still dealing with that East vs. West Coast beef. The territorial lines were drawn. In a way, that's how No Limit and CMB got their shine.

I'm not gonna say they didn't earn their time in the sun. They did they shit. But a lot of it had to do with the war between Suge and Diddy.

Nevertheless, I was still able to make moves. I was travelling with my cuddies on some Rompilation shit, for real! We was having fun. I was moving so much weight it was sick. On top of that, I kept a bad hoe bitch at my side.

Look... I'm a pimp by blood. Any Country Club Crest representa' got some 'P' in 'em. So even though I was with Noel, on the road I kept a hoe bitch or two around. And I wasn't soft on 'em either.

I remember one night in Miami, me and Stupid Swoop from G-Parkway was riding down South Beach. I was in the passenger seat of that S-Class and the cuddy was in the backseat behind the driver. My lil bitch, Mimi was driving. She kept yawning and shit. Talking 'bout she was tired and needed some rest. Shit, it was only two a.m. and Mimi was lit. If anything, I would've let her sleep in the car while we hit the next club, but she wasn't 'bout to get some rest right then and there. She was the driver.

"Daddy, I'm tired," she said when we pulled up at a red light.

I looked at her and shook my head. She was getting way too comfortable. So I told her to put the car in park. When she did as she was told, I said, "Get out, bitch! Get out an give me twenty-five pushups!"

I don't know what Swoop was thinking 'cause cuddy looked at me like I was crazy. But I wasn't. Never been. She was tired so I woke her game up.

She got out with high heels on along with a short skirt with no panties and started doing pushups right then and there. It was a four-lane avenue so cars were everywhere, coming and going. But that didn't stop her. She did her pushups like a real trooper then got back in the car refreshed.

I was in Atlanta too. Me and 40 patched up our differences by the time the 2000's came. It's not like we hated each other. That Hillside nigga got love for the 707 so his word held weight at the table.

The first time I went to Atlanta was when I met Big Meech. I give it to that nigga. Meech's a real nigga. When it came to powder, him and his brother were like El Chapo in they reach. They had unlimited supply with their plug. And unlimited reach under the cloak of BMF and the music industry.

I could be in Akron, Ohio; if one of the cuddies needed 5 kilos I'd call Meech. Twenty minutes later, I'd get a call by a nigga out there telling me where to go pick up the work. It was the same in Missouri, Texas, Tennessee, Oklahoma and Louisiana. Them niggaz had reach.

Meech was the reason Detroit knew about Thizz Nation. And trust me when I say Detroit isn't an easy City to penetrate. If you try to do a show out there without the proper gangland co-signature you'll see a hundred goonies posted up at the entrance, blocking all your ticket sales.

And if the act actually goes on stage - the same niggaz you saw at the entrance is gonna storm that mothafucka.

There's a lot of Mob controlled areas. But Detroit is one of them places that's ruled with an iron fist. Every city has it's gangland landlords. If you're in the industry, it doesn't matter how big you get, you must pay your respects to the landlord. If not, there's repercussions to your actions. And I repeat, no one is exempt. No matter how big they get. No one is bigger than the program.

By the early 2000's the hyphy movement was in full effect! We were moving hard on some Rompilation shit. I made it. I was nation wide, but there was still a long way to go before I reached my peak...

CHAPTER

TWENTY-NINE

"We had an army that could flood any city in any State at any time of the year."
-Mac Dre

There's different levels to the game, yet the game is still the same no matter where you go. Whenever you step into any major industry, your job is gonna include travelling from State to State. Imposters, niggaz who are really just studio gangstaz aren't going to mix well with authentic vibes because true colors glow wherever you go. Real niggaz shine, though. Especially if you really from a ghetto. It's a give in because most ghettos across America breed a certain breed of nigga.

Field niggaz...

When you become a celebrity in addition to being a made man, your world inevitably gets bigger. You're not only dealing with niggaz in your neighborhood, city, county or State anymore. Suddenly, you're politicking with mob figgaz from all over the country. Especially if you're getting money in someone else's trenches.

That's exactly what happened in Kansas. See... The Mob is a cartel that consists of a bunch of Bay Area factions all working in Cohesion. At home, although we are all one family, we're still individual bosses. But on the road, a Frisco nigga is gonna be thick as thieves with a cat from Sacramento, just as long as everyone involved has mafia ties. It's the beauty of being part of something bigger than you.

It's like this: You might have a cipher of monsters who you terrorize shit with, but there's always going to be circles within circles. Once you're certified, the VIP passes are well known and understood. Nevertheless, aliens, civilians, any sort of outsiders won't be privy to what really goes on behind closed doors.

My situation in Kansas started in '03. Y'all know who Messy Mary is, right? Mess is from Frisco. He was a made man way before me, so he had all the plugs I had. He was in Kansas pushing powder.

Mess is a Damu. He was fucking with a nigga named Tone who was from a Crip set out there in Kansas. I think he was from a set that repped 51st Street. Don't get the locale twisted, either. A lot of people tend to underestimate out the way places like Kansas, Omaha, Alabama, Kentucky, Arizona and all that. I'm telling you, the hood is the hood no matter what city or State you're in. A nigga from Wisconsin will kill you just as quick as someone from Los Angeles if they're given the right reason.

So, let's move on. In Kansas there was a young nigga named Fat Tone who had his shit together. He was running his set on some goon shit. They were taking shit over by force. Pushing a hard line on everyone in their city.

The nigga, Mess had did a show out there with Killa Tay and was tryna bust a few plays while he was out there. Like I said, Mess was connected. He had plugs for anything he wanted. This allowed him to broker deals wherever he went. In case you don't understand how that works, let me explain it...

At the time, kilos of coke were going for 20 G's a piece to niggaz who had access to them. In the early 2000's, Atlanta was the hub. Miami and L.A. had lost it. They had it too but BMF were the bigger than anything else going on at the time. The further away from Atlanta you were, the higher the coke prices were.

If you were part of the inner circle, you could get bricks for something like 16 or 17k. With that type of plug, you could go to somewhere like Seattle where kicks were going for 24k. But, I couldn't call the people who had it in Seattle. I had to call Meech or his brother, Terry and they'd do what they had to do to get that shit dropped in my lap. Then I'd turn around and sell whatever I had to whoever I sold it to. This allowed me and everyone else with the plug to travel from State to State and still be able to conduct business without having to traffic across State lines.

As we travel across the country on tours, we meet people. We meet club promoters who know the local ballers and that's how we get around. Networking. Mess had it like this too.

Mess and Tay were fucking with this nigga, Fat Tone. Fat Tone brokered a deal for five bricks where he was supposed to make five racks profit for serving someone from his city who Mess and Tay didn't know. They'd done business before and everything was all good until it wasn't. On this specific round, the guys who Fat Tone did the deal with said three of the two kicks sold to them were fake. Straight sheet rock! They didn't know Mess and Tay like that, cause Tone never introduced them. He had been the face of the deal. So the Kansas niggaz pressed up on Tone. Since the product had came straight from Mess's hands to Tone's hands Tone automatically assumed Mess robbed him.

The Kansas hustlers blamed Tone. Tone blamed Mess. Since all this was found out after Mess left Kansas, most of the dispute took place over phone calls instead of in person.

Mess was on some other shit. He didn't respect Fat Tone and his people. He not only refused to listen to their gripes, he was on some hot shit by riding around their city in a Maserati. One thing got to another and the Kansas niggaz who felt like they were robbed found Mess, Tay and Fat Tone in traffic and they started drillin'. Shooting Fat Tone in the process.

Let me explain something to y'all real quick: If a made man gets shot or killed, it's a big deal. There's gonna be retribution and major repercussions. We had an army that could flood any city in any State at any time of the year. So, yeah, we had street marines with experience in guerilla warfare but violence isn't always the best option. A problem can be handled with finesse if you have the right player at the table. It's as simple as that.

Mess could've let the hounds loose if he had chosen to. Them Frisco niggaz push a hard line too. They got heavy metal with long dicks. They live like that on a daily basis. But he didn't call for his soldiers. Instead, he packed up and left. I don't have enough information on anything else that took place prior to him leaving, so I'm not gonna speak on it any more. But the fact is he left some loose ends.

Some deadly loose ends...

Fast forward a year. It's Halloween of '04. Me and the louies were at a club in Kansas doing a walk-through. For those of you who don't know what a walk-through is, it's when you get paid to show up and hang out at a night club. You ain't gotta perform either. Just be there for a few hours and party. Whenever I do a walk-through, I have extra fun. It's like

I'm getting paid to go dumb. We weren't too deep that night either. It was me, Fab, Mac Minister, Dubee, Swoop and a few other fellaz. We were popping thizz, drinking lean and smoking real big. I was getting paid to do it big.

The premise of a walk-through is like hiring a social media influencer to push your product. Remember... the masses are sheep. An influencer wears a certain shirt and the sheep will go out and buy it too. Same game different concept. When you're hot and you show up at a club, people will go to that club to hang out with you. Even when you're not there, they wanna feel like they got access to where the stars shine.

So that night we went to the club and Fat Tone was there. I knew of him, but I never really fucked with him before. Nevertheless, he was in the circle, so we was all at the club together.

The club we were at had an upper level with about four tables that were a VIP section. It overlooked the dance floor. Yet, at the same time it was eye to eye with the stage and DJ Booth. We was all up there chillin'.

At one point throughout the night, Fat Tone brought up the bullshit with Mess. That shit took place a whole year earlier, but he wasn't letting it go for nothing in the world.

"That shit ya' boy did was fucked up," Tone said.

"First of all, I don't know who *Ya' boy* is and second, I have no idea why you brining it to me," I had told him, feeling irritated that I had to hear about that bullshit.

"I'm talking 'bout Mess and Tay. Them niggaz got me shot."

"That's unfortunate, P. But, yeah the club poppin' and I'm tryna take one of these bitches back to the room-"

"Dre, you not hearing me," he continued persistently.

I really wasn't trying to hear shit that nigga was talkin' 'bout, to keep it 100 with you.

"I hear ya'," I told him. "But you ain't saying shit. Look, bruh: I don't do all the talkin' behind people's back. If it's news I need to know, my cuddies will bring it up at a table top discussion. That shit you got going on with whoever you got it going on with ain't got nothing to do with me."

"You from the Bay Area, right?"

"Damn right!" I snapped. I wasn't feeling the direction his convo' was heading towards. "So, what you getting at?"

"I had to pay them niggaz outta my own bread 'cause that slob-ass nigga, Mess gave me some fugazi shit. So, that means somebody from Cali is gonna have to give me my money."

Now, he had my attention. I wasn't a gang banger, but I understood the language. I looked at him directly in the eyes and calmly stated, "I told you that shit ain't got nothing to do with me. But, you know what... As a matter of fact, what'chu wanna do? Your tone is getting real hostile."

"You know Gary?" he asked.

I thought to myself, *That's the promoter that got me the walk-through.*

"Cuz from the 50's."

"And what that mean?"

"It means y'all ain't getting paid 'til I get mines. No Bay Area artists is getting' Kansas money 'til I get mines!"

Tone was making a bold statement. He was an idiot if he thought I was gonna let that ride. If I even entertained that sort of jazz, not only would my affiliates deal with me accordingly, but it would open the door for all kinds of shiesty shit to go down.

Robbing niggaz for their show money is a regular hustle for some promoters. It all goes back to when I was telling y'all about a studio gangsta's glow. If you're team wasn't known for breaking jaws or shooting shit some of the harder promoters will rob you for your payment every time.

They got all kinds of tricks. They'll tell you they got robbed. If you split the door money, they'll short you by half. Sometimes, they'll tell you the drinks are free, then at the end of the night they hit you with a bill in the thousands for some watered down shit.

Then you got the niggaz who're certified gorillas. Them niggaz will recognize if you soft or not. And if they sense any sort of weakness they'll just take your money. You might not even leave the city with your jewels.

The gorilla type of niggaz capitalize off the fact that most rappers don't wanna cross State lines with an arsenal. They also know they got the home team advantage, they got you outnumbered and outgunned so they try and muscle certain rappers every chance they get.

This is why real niggaz touch base with the local landlords. But, then again, sometimes that leads us into situations like the one I found myself in with that nigga Fat Tone. Tone was a boss in his city. He was a leader of men and he was flexing his muscles that night.

Here's the thing about me, though. I'm a man before I was a rapper. I was a Country Club Crest reresenta' from the crib. The Romper Room don't breed suckaz! I'll be damned if I ever let a nigga disrespect me. It don't matter what the odds are!

"You ain't getting paid for this job, Dre. Real talk! And if you got a problem, there's 50 crips in here that'll help you get ya' mind right!"

This nigga really got up like he was finna get away with that. By then I saw red! I grabbed that Crystal bottle and smacked that sucka upside his head! My nigga Dubee swung on that fool's homeboy and the rest of the cuddies went up!

The opposition wasn't 50 deep but they was thick! That nigga Fab was at the door getting our bread as it came in. He was strapped so he was alright. And if it would've gotten too spicy in that bitch he would've equalized everything for us.

Meanwhile, we was throwing blows with Tone's crew. I climbed on top of that nigga, tryna knock his teeth out with every blow. Then, BAM! I got kicked in the head. I stumbled and that fuck-boy got up. We locked like pits! I could tell he was raised in the trenches 'cause he was fighting just as hard as I was.

I had hands and was known to K.O. mothafuckaz. My jaw ain't soft, either. I can take 'em just as hard as I can give 'em. Me and that fool locked horns like beasts!

We exchanged blows, one after another. Oblivious to our surroundings, we ended up tumbling down the stairs. There was a sea of blue rags and big butts down there. Me and this nigga was blammin' each other with some hay makers. Then Swoop did some shit that gave all of us an open line to the door. Cuddy grabbed a champagne bottle off someone's table and smashed one of Tone's homies in the mouth so hard, the whole club heard the smack. That shit knocked damn near every tooth at that nigga's mouth. At least that's what it looked like when all them teeth came flying out his shit.

Anyways... that shocked everyone. Mothafuckaz stopped in they tracks. Frozen in time.

That gave us the opening we needed to get the fuck up outta there.

We bounced! I don't know how he did it but Dubee had gotten the Van we was in pulled around front of the club. We skirted up outta there real quick.

Before we got on the highway we stopped at a Chevron station to clean up. I had blood all over

me. My lip was busted too but that wasn't shit.

The good news was Fab got the money. He told us when the fighting started he pulled out his hammer and took the whole bag from the nigga who was collecting it with him. It was about 12 bands altogether. I took thirty-five hundred and the cuddies split the rest. For us, it was just another night in the game. We'd have to watch ourselves 'cause I still had a thizz deal to handle out there the next morning. Which meant we still had to stay in Kansas another night.

All in all, that shit did have me hot. In my eyes, it was Mess's fault. He was gonna have to give me a fade for that shit. The whole situation was on him and his unresolved business. Regardless, nothing was gonna get handled that night so we cleaned ourselves up, hopped back in the van and hit the highway.

CHAPTER
THIRTY

"Let 'em pull up, blood! Real talk, I'll empty this bitch!"
-Mac Minister

I made sure to get me some orange juice and Skittles before we hit the road. That OJ go crazy with thizz. Anyways, I looked in the backseats of the van and saw all the cuddies mean muggin' an shit. We were definitely outnumbered in that club, but we made it out alive, with all the door money. In my eyes, that was a win.

"What-da-fuck wrong wit' y'all?" I asked the cuddies. "This nigga, Fab got us fucked up tonight."

"What?" asked a surprised Mista Fab.

"If we would've been riding in that short bus you always talking 'bout we probably would've had helmets on and I wouldn't have gotten my lip busted!"

"What?!" the group busted out. "Ahh- hell naw! Ain't nobody wearing no mothafuckin' helmets!"

Finally, the mood was lifted. That's what we all needed. In all actuality, a brawl in a club wasn't shit. Regardless of the reason, no one was shot and killed so it wasn't all that bad. We lit up some blunts, turned up the music and let the windows down so we could feel the breeze that only comes when you're speeding through life.

The situation at the club needed to be addressed. But it was slowly creeping it's way out of my mind to make room for the weed smoke. That was until Swoop got a call...

"What's good... Oh, yeah... Yeah, fuck 'dat nigga... A'ight! Bet!"

After ending the call, I heard him say, "Dre."

The tone of his voice told me I was about to hear some shit.

"What's upper, cuddy?"

"This little Indian thang I met the other night just tapped in. She was at the club just now."

I turned down the music to hear him better.

"She knows Fat Tone. And she talking 'bout that bitch-ass nigga took off with some of his goonies and they coming our way."

Mac Minister pulled out a Glock with an extendo. "Let 'em pull up, blood! Real talk, I'll empty this bitch!"

"Fuck 'dem niggaz," I told them. "Call baby back and tell her we gonna go get 'er in the morning. Make sure she got some other hoes with her too!"

"That's right!" Dubee agreed. "Life goes on, bitch!"

If I would've taken them niggaz seriously I would've had Dubee turn the mothafuckin' van around so we could blitz 'em. The best way to handle a situation like that is to cut all loose ends where they hang at. But, I made the mistake of not classifying the incident as a life or death predicament.

A part of me didn't blame Fat Tone for what happened. If I would've been robbed, or felt like I was robbed it would've been duck hunting season on mines. On-my-momma, there was a time in my life I probably would've done the same shit he did. Especially before I was inducted into the Mob.

I was more than willing to let that shit go until the facts were investigated more closely. If Mess was wrong, we would've dealt with it diplomatically. But if that nigga, Fat Tone did some dumb shit like sending shots at the Mob to cover his own sins then there'd be no understanding whatsoever.

I was just getting back into my groove when someone in the back said, "Check this out, y'all!"

"What's crackin'?" I asked them.

Suddenly, Minister, Fab and Swoop went to my side of the van and looked out the window. Somebody was approaching us on my side. One of them yelled, "Dre!"

YACKA! YACKA! YACKA! YACKA! YACKA!

Shots were coming from a black Infiniti. The cuddies started bustin' back!

Bladadah! Bladadah! Bladadah!

Glass shattered!

The van swerved!

The gunshots were loud! The winds was stinging my face! The bus swerved to the right, then left! Glass was flying everywhere. A piece got in my eye.

The Infiniti was right next to us. Right next to me. A nigga with a strap was bustin' from the backseat. The driver was too! Then I saw Fat Tone. He was hanging out the passenger window leaning over the top of the car with his gun pointing directly towards me. We made eye contact.

Everything was fast, loud and cold until...

Until I felt something sharp hit me in the neck. I reached for the spot that was burning and my hand came back red.

"Cuddy, I'm hit!" I yelled, but no sound came out of my mouth. I remember thinking, *Damn! Did they shoot my voice box out?*

Then the world turned upside down. The van we were in flipped and rolled. That's when things started slowing down. I saw the cuddies lose their grip on things. I hit the ceiling, the door, then back into my seat before suddenly smashing into the windshield.

Everything changed after I hit the windshield. That's when I started seeing shit. I was at a dice game...

It looked like my momma's garage...

Then I was in the passenger seat of a Cutlass...

Me and the cuddies were racing through the Crest. The Louie took a hard left and suddenly the Cutlass was gone...

We were running through some bushes. On the other side of the bush there was a fence...

I was alone now...

I hit the fence and jumped...

Within a blink of an eye, I found myself in a hotel room. Diggs and Curt were laughing. Some Mexican bitches were walking around butt naked...

Everything felt unsteady while I was experiencing those visions. Almost as if everything was happening amidst a earthquake. Then suddenly, it all stopped. I was surrounded by a gang of niggaz in prison uniforms. A riot had kicked off. Mothafuckaz was running to and fro, throwing blows while swinging knives...

A gunshot...

A head splattered...

The visions were happening fast, but then they weren't. Time felt weird. Kinda like it didn't matter anymore. I know it might not make sense when I say time stopped meaning shit, but that's the best way I can explain what happened; how it all felt at the time.

It was starting to get hard to breathe. I felt like I was drowning, yet my mouth was dry. All of a sudden, I saw my momma's face. She reached for me but then she disappeared...

I saw Noel. She smiled at me before fading away...

Next, I was on a stage at a club in Hawaii...

At a sideshow...

Sideshow after sideshow. Cars were doing donuts, smoking up the streets...

There was energy coursing through my veins. I felt hyphy! It was real! It was a part of me!

And then it left…

I was gone. I was dead. It was weird, but I knew it. My soul had left my body. I felt like energy. Static electricity. I couldn't feel my head, arms, legs or any other part of my body. But I could still see shit.

On-my-momma, I was spooked. It was unreal. Imagine suddenly feeling like everything you've ever known about life no longer being real. I saw the cops. The ambulances. The cuddies throwing their guns into a far off field.

Then I saw me…

I didn't move when the EMT's put that white sheet over my body. It was over.

I was dead…

CHAPTER
THIRTY-ONE

"Fear had been a part of my life for as long as I can remember."
-Mac Dre

A lot of people watch what they're saying when they know they're being watched. They pay attention to their words because not all conversations are supposed to be shared with everyone. I realized a long time ago that the world is a stage. You're always being watched especially when you don't think you are.

It took me some time to get used to the state of being I'm in. I no longer reside in my body so there are certain feelings (physical) I don't feel anymore. I do feel something though. I know my essence is intact. It feels like I'm a ball of energy that can't be seen, heard or felt.

There's two things I learned about death. I can chill and maintain a peaceful state of nothingness. Or, I can let myself get pulled towards vibes. It seems like my essence is attracted to places where people are thinking about me. If someone is thinking of me hard enough, I'll just show up where they're at. If there's a group of individuals channeling my energy at one place at one time it'll transport me to wherever they at.

At first, it was fucked up 'cause I was pulled towards my family and friends. Time doesn't make sense anymore. That, I can't explain in words. A year can seem as long as ten minutes. Ten minutes can go as slow as a year. When you're in the same room as your momma and she's crying, it can literally feel like it'll never end. Especially when all you wanna do is hug her and let her know you're right there with her - but you can't...

I've had a lot of time to think about shit since I've been gone. One of the subjects I've really chewed on was emotions I no longer felt. The biggest one was fear. In death, there's no such thing as fear. It just doesn't exist in this realm.

In life, fear had been part of my life for as long as I can remember. I remember being a kid and terrified of my mother whooping my ass. She had a list of infractions the six and seven year old me would get whooped for.

My ass was in danger of getting stung by a belt, extension cord or sandal for being too loud when she was tired; if I broke a toy she just bought me; if I got caught jumping on the bed; she'd threaten to whoop my ass if I came in the house crying after having a fight with some other kids. She'd whoop my ass if I tore up a new pair of shoes too quick. Or, if I spoke her 'business' to some social workers or Section 8 representatives. I'd get threatened if I didn't finish my dinner or got a bad grade at school.

As I got older, the fear of my momma's threats no longer held the weight it had when I was a child. To the world, the teen Dre was fearless. Catching a fad; committing a felony to get paid; or busting that heater at a sucka was nothing. But, the whole time, in the back of my mind the major equalizer was death. Although, it didn't change anything, after The Mac was taken from us, I always knew death was real.

There's thousands of ways you can lose ya' life in the ghetto. Someone could've killed me at a house part. I could've been caught lackin' for thinking I was cool with the wrong nigga. My life could've been taken for being too extra on the avenue. Could've even lost my life during a heist, or by the hands of a pig.

Any one, two or three of those things could've happened to me before my 21st birthday. But it didn't. Mac Dre made it through the game, prison and into the music industry as a made man!

Here's the cold part about life that most people fail to understand until it's too late. Even though death is always lingering, especially when you're in the game, the fear never really goes away. As my career exploded, I still worried about other things. I worried about what people thought about me and my push. I had to. Everyone saw the hyphy movement grow. I was on top of the world and I was being watched by everyone.

All the money got me to thinking too. I thought about what it would've been like if I lost it all. There were a few times when I'd get so high I was outta my body, I thought the money was fake. It couldn't have been real. Then that would fuck me up, 'cause it got me to wondering where I'd be without it.

There were months when I wouldn't spend shit. Not a dime! While the cuddies were buying houses and cars, I leased shit 'cause I was afraid of what would happen if I spent all my money and had to go back to the trenches.

Don't get me wrong, I love the ghetto. The Crest is where my heart's at. And I made sure to teach all the cuddies that were real fans were the heart of the ghetto.

Going back to the hood, per se, wasn't my actual fear. I feared what came with it. I didn't wanna go back to them mustard and mayonnaise sandwiches.

The days with no electricity and the fridge being empty is what had me traumatized. I'll never forget all the different niggaz my momma let spend the night when the bills were due. All those reasons were why I worked so hard to build my brand.

In the end, none of any of that mattered. I was dead. And everything that happened on earth stayed on earth. I didn't take my fears with me. But I did take my anger!

I saw the candle light vigils. I watched the cuddies cry. I watched the fans cry. I even saw my mother cry. All that shit had me steaming. I couldn't believe I was taken from all that I had built. I was on the verge of really making it big and it was all taken away in a blink of an eye. All over some bullshit I had nothing to do with!

For a long time, the louies were calling me the Bay Area's GOAT. They told me I raised a whole generation. In so many ways, I didn't believe them. In my head, it wasn't my skills that had me on that trajectory. It was my work ethic. My authenticity. My energy. My vibe.

Then it hit me... If all the attributes that I called mine were what made so many people love me - then it was me! If someone was digging my swagger... and my swag was authentic... then it was *ME* who they were feeling!

That shit truly destroyed me for a minute. I was angry because I left everything I spent my life working towards. Still, death gives you a certain level of peace. Eventually, after accepting the state you're in death erases the anger and hate you came with. All the things that once mattered when you were alive stop holding so much weight in the afterlife. At first, it does. But after a while you become a bystander like you're watching the universe unfold.

Now I understand why my Thizz videos sold so much. The world loves reality TV. Even in death, the world is like a big ass reality TV show. And you're right there, front and center, whenever your energy is summoned towards.

One time, it took me to meeting of the bosses at a bar I used to hangout at in Sacramento called Cheers. Ever since I had relocated to Sac, Cheers had become one of my favorite hangouts. To have this meeting that included all the Bay Area bosses at was an ode to me in the highest degree.

Cheers is your typical sports bar and grill. It's in South Sacramento. All the real street niggaz fucked with it back then. The fact that it was located on a certified blade kept the players and pimps in there too. Basically, it's the epicenter of the culture. A little spot where only the real ones congregate.

It was in the morning when the Mob started showing up. The outside of Cheers looked like a car show. The whole parking lot was bumper to bumper with foreign vehicles. The Benzes, Beemers, Vettes and Hummer just showed the class of niggaz that were in attendance that morning.

Inside, it looked like a Bay Area award ceremony, but without the bitches. C-Bo, E 40, Too Short, Stone Ramsey, J Diggs, Kilo Curt, Mall, Coolio, Jacka, Berner, J-Stalin and too many others to list were all there. Most of them were the type of niggaz whose names would never be on a music album. They only lurked in the shadows.

Big Bruh was one of the niggaz the public would never know about. He was there and he was the one who called the meeting to attention.

Niggaz had moved all the tables out the way making it a standing room only affair.

"A'ight," he began. "It's been some weeks since Dre's murder. All kinds of rumors and accusations been thrown out there since shit went South. I know there's a lot of us in here, but everyone's certified so we can all speak freely."

Everyone there knew one another, yet I didn't see one smile.

"Right now, I wanna hear from someone who was actually there the moment Dre died. I don't want rumors, nor assumptions. Straight facts! I think everyone in this room wants to know what really, really took place that night."

There were a few murmurs throughout the crowd. It took a moment, but then Diggs spoke up...

"I already know who did this 'cause I was right there. You already know who did it because I've holla'd at most of y'all individually. But, just to get it out there better you can also hear it from the other cuddies who were there that night."

Jay looked at Swoop and Dubee and told one of them to take the stage.

Stupid Swoop stood up in the middle of the crowd. His long dreads were in corn rolls. He looked around, then started: "Look, man, I'm not gonna waste y'all time. Y'all know what it's like during a walk-through. Dre had that bitch poppin'! It was crowded but we were straight, going dumb in the VIP. We was on our hyphy tip when that nigga Fat Tone showed up with his Rolling 50's niggaz-"

C-Bo cut in, addressing the crowd, "Rolling 50's is a Neighborhood set out of Kansas City."

"Yeah, they was deep," Swoop said. "It was 'bout four of us in there. So the nigga, Fat Tone got to talking 'bout Mess robbing some niggaz and that he was gonna take Dre's door money as payment for that debt."

Everyone stared at Mess. He returned the gesture with an icy glare attached.

Swoop continued, "Dre wasn't going for it. He checked the nigga and a fight broke out."

"One on one?" 40 asked.

"Naw. We were outnumbered like 5 or 6 to 1. Dre didn't give a fuck, tho'."

"That's a real 'V' nigga," 40 commented.

"Damn right!" Mall agreed.

"So, it was a big-ass fight. But we made it out the club. Got in the van and took off."

That's when Big Bruh addressed Dubee. "Diggs said you was driving the van. What happened after y'all left the club?"

"I was at the door getting that walk-thru fee as it came in. I didn't trust their promotor from the gate. I met 'im a couple nights before at the show we did and something told me to watch his bitch-ass. I was at the door when Fat Tone showed up-"

"Did he show up with a squad?" Big Bruh asked.

"He was with 'bout eight niggaz. But they was deeper than that. That club was in their hood, so it was a Crip function! That wasn't the first time I had seen Fat Tone that week. He'd been at the shows and every time I saw him I felt some animosity so I knew to watch him from the moment he stepped in the building. That's why I was ready when the fighting started. I knew I'd have to secure the bag."

"How'd you do that?" Too Short cut in and asked.

"I whipped out on the doorman. As soon as I saw the fighting start, I put the toaster to the promoter's neck and grabbed the loot. You know how it's done."

"That's right!" said a few niggaz in the crowd.

E 40 Looked at C-Bo and commented, "That's them Bay boys in action."

Bo nodded in agreement.

Dubee continued, "So, when the cuddies made it out, I already had the ride waiting. Everyone got in and we headed to a gas station right next to the freeway exit. After cleaning up, we split that door money and got on Interstate 71 heading north."

Suddenly, Dubee got quiet. The whole congregation got hush mouthed as well. Everyone could tell the cuddy was holding back tears. Shit was startingto get to him, but he kept going.

"... We was on the highway when an Infinity pulled up on Dre's side."

"Did you see the driver?" Mess asked.

"I saw one of the niggaz. He was in the back passenger seat. They called that nigga Cowboy, if I recall correctly."

That statement caused the group to murmur amongst themselves. Dubee couldn't speak anymore. The louie choked up so Swoop cut in and continued for him.

"Them niggaz in the Infinity started bustin' at us from the passenger side. We started shootin' back, but they had choppers. They were eating the side of the van up. Glass was flying everywhere. I think that's what happened to Dubee. Glass hit him in the face and he lost control. The van flipped and started rolling. When we finally stopped, Dre was unconscious. Cuddy's neck was leaking. We pulled him out the van and tried to wake him up. Then, a little while later, some ambulances came."

That's when everyone went silent. It seemed as if they were all in a trance. Probably thinking about all the dead bodies they'd seen over the years. A few of them had day ones die in their arms before. So there was no telling where their thoughts took them. I could literally see their souls heating up. The group as a whole was past angry. There was hatred in their hearts.

After a while, Big Bruh spoke up and that's when the conversation I had been waiting on started. Big Bruh addressed Mess...

"What happened, brody? What started this shit? And, how did it get so far? From the sounds of it, this whole situation was rooted in a deal gone bad on your end. Am I right?"

Mess looked like a snake amongst snakes. He knew he was at court, yet he didn't show any fear. The lack of fear was understood, but to some, it was interpreted as a lack of remorse for what ended up happening to me.

"Big Bruh," he started. "As a matter of fact, this goes to all of y'all: Especially the Romper Room. I didn't rob them niggaz. We got so many plugs I wouldn't have had to. We all know how shit goes down. I didn't take any work out there. Fat Tone was a middle man for some niggaz he knew out there. So, I got some shit from a Mob tie that has always been official. I served him. Then the next day, this nigga hits me up talking 'bout his partnaz is saying the work wasn't any good. I let 'im know there wasn't no refunds and that got him to start talking slick. I would've taken care of the shit, but I had to do a show in Reno so I didn't have time for the bullshit."

"Why didn't you go back?" Kilo asked.

"Yeah, nigga!" Diggs barked with a murderous stare. "I know the nigga had to have been blowing up your phone if he though you robbed him."

"He did. And I told him I had him on the next round. I was gonna take care of everything. Me and Tone talked about it and everything was cool."

"You didn't work it out, nigga!" Dubee spat venomously.

Marv got real disrespectful next...

"You need to watch 'dat tone you using, blood. I didn't know all'at shit was gonna happen!"

"Fuck all 'dat!" hissed Dubee.

Then Diggs cut in, "I need that, bitch-ass nigga!"

"Me too!" echoed Mall.

"I do too!" demanded Stupid Swoop.

Then Big Bruh spoke up: "Check this out, y'all. We all loved Dre. I know there's underlying issues that need to be dealt with, but that's not what we here for. We know Fat Tone did something outta pocket and this is what's on the table. So slow your role so we can take care of one thing at a time."

To the group, he said, "Fat Tone is a crip. Meaning he got a hood behind him. What I need to know, is it necessary to burn his whole neighborhood down or is this an isolated issue?"

Everyone looked at Messy Mary since Mess had the most experience dealing with Fat Tone's set.

Marv said, "Naw. We take him out and I don't see any retribution. But we gonna have to take that nigga Cowboy out too. That's his main gunna. And his word holds weight too."

"No problem!" Swoop stated.

Big Bruh addressed the group again, "Does everyone agree with this?"

Every head in the bar nodded in response.

Then, to Mess he said, "Okay. Marv, this hit is on you-"

"Big Bruh," J Diggs cut in. "With all due respect, Dre was my best friend. All of us who're reppin' the Romper Room loved that nigga. This one's gotta be on us. We gotta take this one."

"I got hitters ready," Marv said.

"Shut-da-fuck-up, bitch-ass nigga!" Kilo growled.

"Fuck you!" he snapped back.

"Enough!" bellowed Big Bruh. Then, specifically towards Diggs he said, "You sure?"

"Yeah. I've never been more sure of anything in my whole life. And, I think I speak for the whole Crest when I say we need that from Mess's bitch-ass."

"It's whatever on mines!" Mess barked as he started taking off his shirt.

"You getting real mouthy over there, my weebles," 40 Water added.

"He is acting real disrespectful, ain't he," Too Short interjected.

"What?" Mess said.

"Whaaap!" Kilo caught Mess in the jaw with a hard right. Suddenly niggaz started moving out the way. Kilo and Mess locked up, exchanging blows.

While that fight was going down, J Diggs swung on Killa Tay.

When the niggaz who had came to the meeting with Mess looked like they were about to jump, 40 stepped in and said, "Check this out, loved ones. Dre was everyone's guy. But these was his day ones. There's things that need to be aired out, Mob ties or not. So y'all need to tuck them fists back in them pockets or it's gonna get extraordinarily gruesome in this bitch."

"He ain't neva' lied!" C-Bo Barked.

That's when the rest of the louies got involved. Swoop, Dubee, Mall and Coolio jumped into the squabbles that were taking place. It was 6 against 2! Fists were flying from every coast. Niggaz were throwing haymakers! Blood flew every where with every loud "Smack!" sound you heard.

Mess and Tay got an authentic Romper Room ass whoopin' that day. I felt the energy too. It was deep anger rooted in their hearts. And they were letting it out with every punch thrown. That ass whoopin' wasn't just about dishing out pain, it was about alleviating it too. I could read their hearts. It's hard to explain how you can understand energy in death, but you just can. It's a different language but it comes through and is understood automatically.

That's how I knew they knew whoopin' Mess and Tay wouldn't bring me back. Nevertheless, they needed the relief. With every punch they threw I felt a tear go down my cuddies faces. They loved me, but they needed to feed. They craved blood.

The louies beat Mess and Tay down, but they didn't stomp them out. That's not what that was about. The truth of the matter was that everyone present that day knew the one guaranteed certainty of the game was its definite uncertainty. No one can expect a specific reaction to any action made in the streets. There's just too many variables to be able to predict where all the cards will fall in any specific situation. Still, the louies needed to get that off their chests and that's exactly what they did...

CHAPTER THIRTY-TWO

"Regardless of who is involved, every plan depends on the Mark reacting accordingly with the plays he's presented with."
-Mac Dre

One of the biggest perks of being a member of the Mafia is the wisdom that's bestowed upon you by other bosses. Not only does working with sophisticated groups of criminals give you a leg up on the deaf, dumb and blind, it also gives you other perspectives of every scenario that's presented to you. That's exactly what took place behind closed doors after I lost my life.

The cuddies wanted to be hands on when it came to sliding on my behalf. There was nothing wrong with that. I would've felt and reacted the same exact way. The problem was the louies were too emotionally involved with the whole situation. Their vision as a collective was clouded by the rage fueled by their need to take revenge on my killers.

I could see their emotions. They wanted to walk straight into Fat Tone's momma's house, hold her hostage and have her call Tone to come meet his death. Tone's family was very close to being murdered. Every single person in his immediate family was in danger at one point throughout the planning process. The only reason it didn't go down like that was because the Cuddies decided it would've been too sloppy. Everyone would've easily connected a massacre of that scale to what had happened to me. Big Bruh along with a few other OG's sat the louies down to explain why they couldn't kill Tone's whole bloodline.

Jay and Diggs were at a studio in Downtown Sacramento about a week after the stomp out convention at Cheers. The engineer had left them alone in front of the mixing board, giving them space knowing they needed to have a private conversation.

"... I know," Curt said. "We gotta make Fat Tone feel safe. We need to rock 'im to sleep. If not, we might never catch 'im in the open."

"What you saying?"

"Maybe we need to go holla at his people. Let 'em thin we not trippin'."

"Or... We can not say shit. Give him some time to think it's all good. Then, he'll eventually come out on his own."

"Yeah. That's how a nigga will usually handle shit. But the bro's said some real shit. Nigga's can't leave nothing to chance. We gotta play chess, not checkers."

"I know. I know... We gotta do this in a way where everyone knows we did it. But nobody can prove we did it."

"On mommas, cuddy! That's some real shit. Dre would've done it the same mothafuckin' way! But, either way, I just wanna split that bitch head. It doesn't matter how it's done."

As far as I was able to watch things go down, they stuck to their plan too. Curt sent Fat Tone messages through third parties telling him nobody from out our way thought he had anything to do with my Death. Diggs took it a step further by speaking on it in different interviews. Every time he was asked about it, he'd say shit that led the sheep to believe Tone was the last person suspected.

The next step of their plan was to bring Tone's shooter out into the open. The catch was, it couldn't just be anywhere. Someone needed to lure Tone and his nigga, Cowboy to the right place at the right time. That part fell on Mess since he was an affiliate who fucked with him in the past.

I love the louies. While all this was playing out, the cuddies were gettin' more and more amped. They already knew they'd eventually catch Tone. One night, when I was magnetized towards their energy they were arguing over who was gonna be the trigger man. They all wanted to have the honor of snatching Tone's soul from his body.

In the end, they agreed on the shooter. It was gonna be Mac Minister. He was from Frisco. He was a known hitman who dubbed as a promoter. The nigga was sharp. A real professional.

Most people don't realize promoters are some of the hardest niggaz in the industry. Promoters are the guys who can get you into any venue in their zone. They also make sure your show gets sold out. If you go to Houston and you're from out of State, you probably won't know a lot of people out there. Not enough to sell out an arena. That's why you'll need someone local. Someone with the right connections in that City. A good promoter will make sure the only thing you gotta worry about is performing. He'll make sure all the tickets get sold and you get paid.

Here's the catch though: Some promoters are certified thugs. They pose as legitimate business men but they're actually professional extortionists. If you don't go through them, your show can get sabotaged in a few different ways.

I'm telling you - there's a nigga in Detroit who will have 100 goonies at the gate making sure no one gets in. If you go into Detroit without checking in with bruh - the show will NOT go on...

Since these types of promoters are natural born hyenas they are trained in the art of sniffing out suckaz. I can't begin to name all the soft-ass rappers I know who have been robbed by promoters. The promoter will set up the whole show. Make sure it's sold out. Collect the money. Then blatantly rob the studio gangsta who did the show. That's the real reason rappers who are real street niggaz push with a squad of hyenas of their own. It's a way of not only showing force - it's also - being a force!

There's also promoters who spread their wings and push cross country. To be a promoter like this, you need a mouthpiece that allows you to network well with people from other regions. You really gotta be a Master at Communicating with people. And that's

what Mac Minister was. He was the type of nigga you could call to connect the dots that you don't have access to. Add that in with the fact that he was a real street nigga and you had one dangerous fella.

Regardless of who is involved, every plan depends on the mark reacting accordingly with the plays he's presented with. Fat Tone wasn't stupid. Anyone with eyes, ears and an ounce of brain could tell I was a made man by the impact my death had on the West Coast.

I'll never take from any man's gangsta no matter what the circumstances may be. From what I saw, Tone knew he fucked up. He knew he had a bag on his head. At the same time, the nigga is one of 'dem boyz in his city. He's got a few notches on the handle of his hammer. Not only that, the nigga also has a brigade of Neighborhood Crips following his orders. Niggaz who would die for him just as quick as they would kill for him. That's the plain truth of the matter. He was the man in his section.

One of his weaknesses was his ignorance of the Mob's reach. See... a lot of niggaz go their whole lives without leaving the four block radius of their stomping grounds. In theory, they can imagine Bentley's, G5's and overseas kilo transactions. But in reality they lack the mental capacity to grasp those types of things.

A limited mindset can hinder you in many ways. It'll stop you from understanding how small the world really is. That kind of short sightedness can limit the actual execution of your goals an aspirations. It will blind your judgement. In Fat Tone's case, it made him move like he was bigger than he really was.

Fat Tone did have a head on his shoulders. He moved with a Machiavellian mindset. The nigga actually took over his set by knocking down a factor from his hood named R.L. R.L. wasn't the only nigga he killed, either. Fat Tone was a shooter so I could see how he came to believe he was untouchable.

The problem with that is you can't just go around killin' just any pasta-linguini eatin' mothafucka like myself without having made a deal with the Devil himself. Made men can't be touched without clearance. It's facts.

I still don't fully understand this death shit a hundred percent. I know my energy is attracted to people who think about me. Maybe if I could eat a few double-stacks and wash 'em down wit' some OJ I'd be able to crack the code. But something tells me when a nigga kills you, you're glow is connected to theirs in some way. I never once heard Tone say my name out loud. Yet, I was able to see him anytime I wanted to. He was the one person I could channel effortlessly.

I'm not sure when. It could've been three days or five months when I saw Tone go into his momma's house while she was there with his baby momma. He was hyper as fuck, smiling and shit like he just won the lotto. He walked in and went straight to the kitchen and hugged his momma from behind while she was at the stove frying some chicken.

She was surprised and pushed him away, saying, "Boy! What you got going on?"

"I got something to tell y'all!" he said as he took a seat at the table. His girl was in the kitchen too. She sat on his lap like it was all good.

His moms' turned around, wiped her hands on her apron and said, "Spit it out, boy!"

"I'm 'bout to hit the next level of the game, momma! I'm 'bout to be a superstar!"

His girl lit up. Just like any other hoodrat bitch who latched onto a local rapper's jock strap, she'd been waiting to hear some news like that for a while.

"What happened? Tell us!" his girl demanded as she playfully pounded on his chest.

"I'm 'bout to meet up with Snoop Dog!"

"What?!" both women replied.

"I'm getting introduced to Snoop to see if I can go on tour with him. If cuz approves it, I'm gonna open up for on a 55 city tour!"

"Lord!" his mother exclaimed. "The Lord done answered my prayers! All your hard word is finally paying off, ain't it?"

"Yes, momma!"

"Baby, is this for real?" his girl asked just as surprised as his momma was.

"Yeah. I gotta meet up with this promoter in Vegas and he's gonna introduce us. If it goes as it should, I'll give 'im a percentage of my earnings from the tour. But that ain't shit since my career's gonna blow up after that."

"When we leaving?" his baby momma asked.

"Naw, baby. I can't take you on this one."

"Tsst!" she sucked her teeth and rolled her eyes.

"Don't start that mess!" Tone's momma said. "He's gotta take care of business, girl!"

"For real!" Tone agreed with a smile. "I'm making this move wit' Cowboy."

"When?" they asked.

"Tonight."

$$$$$

Meanwhile, in Vegas Mac Minister was at the cuddy's house. We had a cuddy named Corleone who had a spot in Vegas. He was pushing weight out there, but he also had a hoe bitch getting that hoe money for him.

Corleone was certified North Pole affiliate. The louies made sure he was involved especially since he was already stationed in Nevada. They were in Corleone's den when I heard Mac Minister tell him, "I just got off the phone with da fuck-nigga. He's on his way out here right now."

Corleone was rolling a blunt of that sticky shit. It's not like I could taste or smell it, but I halfway felt that body high I used to get when nigga got super blowed. A chopper rested on the coffee table along with Corleone's bag of trees. It was in pieces. The dirty rag and oil told me he was cleaning that bitch for the drill. If I had a face I would've smiled.

Danae, Corleone's hoe-bitch came into the living room and sat down next to her nigga. That little bitch was nasty. She came in with nothing on, but some red panties. The cuddy didn't seem to mind, either. Minister didn't blink an eye. He was on some real player shit too. My niggaz were cut from an imported cloth. It was apparent in their moves.

"Man... I can't wait to rock this nigga, cuddy! On Dre, R.I.P! I'ma do it for da Bay!"

CHAPTER THIRTY-THREE

"I ain't gonna lie, them niggaz went dumb!"
-Mac Dre

"Cuz! This is really happenin'!" Fat Tone told Cowboy in the elevator on their way to the 7th floor. They were accompanied by a breezy they snatched up from the crap table.

"On 50's, cuz! The way you just killed 'em on the tables is how you finna hit 'em in this rap game!"

"So, you're a rapper?" the Meghan Stallion look-alike asked Tone.

"Damn right, baby! I'm the man where I'm from! I'm Fat Tone, bitch!"

That's all she needed to hear, I guess. 'Cause she leaned in and wrapped her arms around his shoulders then whispered in his ear, "I hope your name ain't the only thing that got fat in it."

"Shit, you 'bout to find out in a minute, cuz!"

"Don't threaten me with a good time."

That was about the time the elevator stopped and the doors opened. They stepped out and headed to the room that Tone and Cowboy had gotten a few hours earlier.

Cowboy was a young nigga. At 22, he kept his team with work. He was a pretty boy the Feds had wanted for a minute by then. He had already reached legendary status. His come-up was one of those situations that only happens once every other generation.

Cowboy had grew up getting money. One of his uncles was extra deep in the game throughout Cowboy's childhood so he was watching and learning everything he needed to know in order to be a grade A hustler for as long as he could remember.

His momma's brother was one of the biggest dealers in his city which meant he was born into the dope game. As he got older, he climbed the ranks. It got to the point where he was the point man for picking up his uncle's work from Arizona. One weekend he was given his uncle's whole re-up stash so he could go pick up twenty bricks of that Fish Scale. What happened next was pure luck. When he left State to go pick up the work, the Feds hit his whole hood with a big-ass indictment that took almost every person in his uncle's crew off the streets. When Cowboy came back to his turf with everyone's work there was no one to give it to. They'd all been arrested.

He ended up running for all them niggaz while they were in federal lockup. That put him in position to become the man in his section. But the problem was the Feds were watching the whole time. They were well aware of his situation while it was playing out so he ended up under investigation too. Luckily, Cowboy wasn't blind to his predicament. So when shit started getting shady he went underground. Only showing his face at night or out of town.

Fat Tone was best friends with the nigga. He kept him close because he knew he could be trusted. Even if Cowboy hadn't been there the night I was murdered he would've still been put on the list since he was the closest entity to Tone. He was guilty by association.

As soon as they entered the room the bitch they were with made a beeline to the bathroom. Tone and Cowboy took a spot on the couch and set up shop. The usual chill scene was set out. Weed, drank and some music Was put on. They were enjoying themselves and I was hating every minute of it. I moved around the room totally invisible to them bitch-ass niggaz, wishing I could off them right then and there. But I couldn't so I just watched.

The curtains were wide open, giving them a view of the nightscape. Vegas had a lot to admire after the sun went down. I had to take some time to admire the scene myself. I've always had a thing about beautiful views from high up places. On some real shit, something told me to take it all in because death was unpredictable. I didn't know what would come from moment to moment. What if I was never given another view like that one...

Tone started counting the money he won at the tables while his boy rolled some trees into a Swisher. The nigga was feeling himself since he won something like three or four bands. I don't blame 'im, it was free money. Even though he wasn't gonna be able to take it with him where he was heading.

After a while passed, baby came out the bathroom looking like she was ready for whatever. "Y'all ready for some drinks?" she asked them in a seductive voice. Her demeanor was smooth, as if she'd done it a thousand times.

"Damn right!" they replied.

I took a moment to study the chick. She was bad. I'll give it too her. A sexy redbone with green eyes and long black hair. Most of her looked authentic too. The curls in her mane told me she was mixed with something Caribbean. Even her lips were real and I loved that extra detail.

I've never been a hater. I'll give niggaz they roses when they deserve them. Even if they're bitch-niggaz like Tone and his sidekick. With that said, I gotta say they were on some player shit. The scene was one I had experienced a million times during my lifetime.

It didn't take them long to get baby out of her clothes. Just like me and the louies would've. They already had a bottle of Heem, but they kept taking the small liquor bottles out the room's fridge adding to the vibe. They were getting more and more bent by the second. Then the real festivities kicked in.

Cowboy and Tone got up and approached the breezy as she danced her two step in front of them. She was with it too. She grabbed Tone by the chain and started kissing him in the mouth.

Cowboy took his position in the rear. He immediately started rubbing her booty. Baby didn't give a fuck, but she was concentrating on Tone. Running her hands across his chest while kissing him like they had known one another for years. Then she switched up. She slowly turned around and started kissing on Cowboy while pushing her ass up on Tone's crotch.

"Bitch, you got ass for days!" Tone said.

"You think you can handle it?" she asked as she maneuvered herself so she was facing both men. The bitch was a pro. She reached down and grabbed both dicks at the same time.

Cowboy said, "Handle that? Man, we finna put you to sleep!"

Using their dicks as grippers she led them both to the couch. Then she took a seat with both of them in front of her. Tone was on her left, his homey on her right. She stared up at both of them like a real porn star as she unbuckled their belts and pulled out their schlongs. She took her time with them niggaz. A sure sign of professionalism.

"Now it's time I show y'all how Vegas girls do thangs," she said before sliding Tone's dick in her mouth.

She licked her lips one last time as she moved them juicy ass dick suckers over the head of his swipe. Her left hand started pumping Cowboy's swipe even harder. Almost at the same exact speed as her head had started bobbing on Tone's crotch.

"That's what I'm talking 'bout, bitch!" Tone moaned. "Give me 'dem brains, baby!"

She closed her eyes while slobbin' on Tone's jock. Over and over, her lips moved up and down his shaft while her right hand held it still. She didn't slow down on Cowboy for one second. She kept pumping that nigga's pipe the whole time she was head-butting Tone's crotch. Then all of a sudden I heard a loud pop sound as she pulled her mouth off Tone's dick.

"Ooohhh-dayum!" he moaned.

Next, she took Cowboy in her mouth and immediately started sucking the soul out of it! The sounds she was making while slurping on his swipe filled the room, overpowering the music that was coming from the television. Even the job she was doing on Tone's dick with her hand was sloppy since it was dripping with spit.

She was doing her shit. But, I've been there before a hundred times with bitches just like her. I could tell she was holding back. After a few minutes of sucking off Cowboy, she switched schlongs and started sucking on his boy. Then she did it again. From dick to dick, she switched back and forth, never missing a beat!

Both of them niggaz were stuck! They stared at her gymnastics like they never seen a bitch demonstrating those types of skills. She was so raw she had drool connected between both swipes! I thought she was gonna let both them niggaz bust in her face but she didn't. She switched gears. She backed up and told them fools, "I want one of these dicks between my tits right now!"

Without any hesitation she took Cowboy's dick and rubbed its head against the center of her chest. Then she let go and grabbed her titties and held them up. Cowboy knew exactly what to do. He took his right hand and gripped her shoulder. Then he took his left hand and put his dick between her titties. Tone backed up and let the scene play out.

She squeezed her titties together and Cowboy went to work. He was humping that bitches chest like a horny dog.

"Yeah! Fuck my titties! Just like that!"

She had a greedy look in her eyes. Every time the head of his dick went through the top of her cleavage she stuck her tongue out to lick it the best way she could.

While this was going on, Cowboy sat down on the couch. That nigga got on the couch and scooted behind the bitch, putting a leg on each side of her. Then he interrupted the sex scene by reaching for her shoulder.

Without saying anything she let go of her titties, grabbed Cowboy's dick and kissed the head. Then she let it go, turned around and straddled Tone. Her knees sunk into the couch. Tone used his right hand to guide his dick into her pussy. That nigga couldn't wait. He was tryna stuff that bitch as fast as he could.

Then, as if sensing Cowboy watching her she reached behind herself with both hands and spread her ass cheeks! Baby, had a fat ass! Real mothafuckin' talk! Even in death, a big booty did something for a nigga! I would've went stupid-doo-doo-dumb in her shit if it was me standing behind her!

Cowboy's bitch-ass was a fool, though. He needed no coaxing. He took his meat in his hand and made that initial thrust into her cheeks. Her eyes closed as she dived into Tone's face and started kissing him roughly. Cowboy spit on her brown eye and kept pushing. Then, suddenly I heard a pop sound and Cowboy's face scrunched up and she pulled up off Tone's lips and yelled, "Ooohhh!"

Tone started laughing.

"You good?" Cowboy asked.

"Damn right!" she replied. "Don't stop! I want both of y'all to fuck me hard!"

Them niggaz kicked into a whole different gear after that. They both went dumb. But I didn't stay there to watch the inevitable explosion of lust that usually wrapped up situations like that. Without realizing it, I was pulled away from their room...

I went from their room to somewhere outside with Mac Minister and Corleone. Minister was leaning against a white Pontiac. They were both sharing a blunt while pouring out some liquor in my honor. It was Grey Goose, I could almost taste it.

"This is for Dre..."

"R.I.P. Dre..."

If I had a body I would've nodded my head. I already knew what vibe they were on. Their energy was both fire hot and grim black.

That nigga, Tone better appreciate his last night on earth, I thought to myself.

By the energy they were emitting it would've been obvious to anyone that they had murder on their minds...

CHAPTER THIRTY-FOUR

"It was as if the night released my glow into the cosmos..."
-Mac Dre

Press play day couldn't have came early enough for me. Tone couldn't wait to meet Snoop. Cowboy was just as hype, feeding off his energy. Meanwhile, Corleone and Mac Minister were putting on their murder faces.

Something I've learned to accept about death is that certain things like physical touch and things like hot or cold no longer exist. You don't have a body so there's no feelings.

Something else that you don't have but it takes time to lose is emotions. At first, I would feel sad about losing my life. There were times my frustrations turned into raging anger too.

Fat Tone was on the phone with his stanking-ass, paddle-body looking bitch expressing his excitement that day. He was hella-extra happy about meeting Snoop. In his eyes, his career was about to explode. Listening to him that morning was one of the last times I felt anger. That shit had me hot! This nigga took me out the game way before I had the chance to reach "Hov" status. And there he was, thinking he was gonna reach the stars.

Bitch-ass-nigga!

If I had one I would've had my thizz face on when he finally got the call from the cuddy. I couldn't wait for the fireworks to play out.

Minister was on his way into the MGM Grand when he made the call. "Tone! What's crackin'? You ready?"

"On Hood, I'm ready! Been up all morning waiting on you, cuz!"

"C'mon down then, homey. Snoop ain't gonna wait on us for too long, that nigga be busy."

"I'll be right down!" Tone replied excitedly. After hanging up, he turned to Cowboy and said, "It's that time, loc! We finna go meet Snoop."

Minister was waiting for them in the lobby when they stepped off the elevator. He greeted them with all the fake love he could muster. I gotta tip my hat to the Mac, he played his part magnificently. I know how hard it must've been for him because I sensed his anger boil the second he saw them. Cuddy was Stanley Steamin'!

What really made me respect that Frisco nigga's gangsta was the way he held himself. Remember, there's a difference between a gangsta and a goon. Gangstaz play chess. They take their time to execute a checkmate. Goons gobble up the opps like checker pieces.

A goon would've knocked them niggaz down right then and there. It wouldn't have mattered how many cameras the lobby had. A goon would've ended up on the news like the time the Hell's Angels and the Mongols were when they kicked it off in the Casino. But, naw... Mac

Minister was on his shit. He was weaving a dangerous web and I loved him for it!

All three of them went outside. Mac was taking them to his car; a blue Tercel. But when they got to it, Fat Tone became hesitant like he didn't wanna get in.

"Cuz," Tone started. "I rented a Magnum. You wanna take that? It's cleaner than this-"

"Oh... You wanna stunt on Snoop, huh?" Minister chuckled.

"Naw-"

"It's good, bruh. I feel you. Appearances are everything in this game. The Magnum seems like the best choice. But on my momma, Snoop ain't gonna pay attention to what we pull up in. He's not gonna be outside. What my concern would be is how his team is gonna act when they see a ride they don't recognize. They know my car. But if we pull up

in some random shit they might not even let us pull in. Feel me?"

"On Hood. Yeah, you right," Tone said.

Tone then looked at Cowboy. Cowboy nodded in agreement and they both got into the Tercel. I sensed the relief in Minister's energy. I already knew why, too. He was taking them bitch-ass niggaz on a one way trip. Taking another car would've complicated things. Not only would he have to worry 'bout disposing the bodies, he'd also have a whole car to worry about too. Not to mention the chance the rental agency had put a tracking device in their vehicle. All those things were loose ends that would add to the drama of getting away so fresh and so clean.

Getting his marks in the car he was driving was really a power move. If shit got hectic and they had their own car they could probably get away a lot easier. Controlling their movements by being their chauffer all played a part in the end game he was setting the stage for.

I'm telling you... Mac Minister was a beast.

On the ride there, brody was blowing their heads up! All the small talk was 'bout Snoop and how he had the means to catapult Tone's career. Minister even went as far as to ask Tone if he was ready to perform if Snoop needed him to show up at the club that night. Both, Tone and Cowboy ate up his cap like it was church sermon.

Mac took them off the strip into a residential area. It wasn't too far off from where Corleone's house was located. For a second, it looked as if they were heading there until he turned in a different direction. He ended up taking them into a subdivision with houses that were in finishing stages of being built. The whole subdivision was still empty, though. It was a ghost-town.

I can't believe Tone and his nigga didn't sense something wasn't right. They pulled up to a house at the end of a cul-de-sac that, in my eyes looked shady-as-fuck. There was a white car in its driveway. Mac Minister pulled in right next to it. It was Corleone's load, a clean-ass Sunbird on chrome thangs.

"Damn," Minister said after turning off the ignition. "He usually leaves the garage open."

"Who?" Cowboy asked.

"Snoop," Tone replied. He was really took by Minister's smokescreen.

Cowboy was suspicious though. It was obvious when he said, "It don't look like anybody lives here, cuz."

"You right," Minister seemed to agree. "Snoop had the whole subdivision built. Holdup, y'all. Let me see what's going on."

Minister was adlibbing by then. I knew this 'cause the garage was 'posed to be open. He knew Corleone was there since his car was in the driveway. But they weren't supposed to be parked outside like that. The plan I heard them put together had them pulling into the garage, then shutting the garage door trapping their marks inside.

Minister was about to step out his car when the garage door started sliding open. They all saw it going up. Then, once it was open they saw Corleone standing there ski-masked up. The cuddy looked like a ghetto Michael Meyers with a chopper in his hand.

"Cuz!" Fat Tone said. "What-da-fuck is this?"

"Hell naw!" Cowboy said.

"Holdup, folks. That's Snoop's dog. Holdup a second. It's good," Minister assured them.

Minister then got up out the car quick as fuck! That's not how the scheme was plotted. But, real talk, I don't think he gave a fuck. I could sense anger brewing in his chest from the moment he met up with them niggaz.

Corleone was extremely emotional as well. He was ready to drill. He didn't miss a beat. He went straight towards the passenger side of their ride. The whole time, he was pointing his 'K' at the targets.

"Get out! Get da fuck out the car, fuck-niggaz!"

Inside the car, Cowboy said, "It's a setup, cuz! The whole time, it was a setup!"

Corleone snatched the passenger door open. That's when shit got mainy for the bitch-ass niggaz! Corleone didn't have a gram of sympathy for either one of them hoes.

BLOCKA! BLOCKA! BLOCKA! BLOCKA! BLOCKA! BLOCKA!

The cuddy squeezed off twenty rounds into Fat Tone's ugly ass! He gave that nigga a facial along with an out of body experience that he'd never come back from. "That's for Dre!" he yelled while drilling holes in the opposition.

Cowboy was tryna get somewhere. He slid out the driver's side of the car. But he wasn't slick. The other homey saw him and started toying with the fuck-boy.

"No-no-nooo," Mac Minister taunted before hitting him with three 40 millimeter slugs to the knee.

Cowboy crumbled. His knee was all over the pavement. He wasn't tryna die, though. That nigga was tryna drag himself down the sidewalk as fast as he could. But he wasn't getting away from the louies. Not that day!

Corleone got greedy. He wanted all the confirmed kills for himself. He quickly rushed around the back of the Tercel and started bustin' at Cowboy like it was legal.

BLOCKA! BLOCKA! BLOCKA! BLOCKA! BLOCKA!

He managed to unload the remainder of the clip knocking Cowboy off his feet for the last time. Then him and Minister stood over his body and started stomping his brains out. They displayed pure bloodlust in that last bit of violence. I could see both of their bodies glowing with rage.

Corleone then turned to Mac Minister and said, "We gotta go!"

"Yeah, I know that! But what we gonna do with the car? You buried that nigga in the Tercel!"

"Fuck the Tercel! We'll call that bitch in stolen!"

"Is you crazy! That shit ain't gonna work! Not with my finger prints all over the steering wheel and shit! I'm not about to hand this mothafucka over to the police like that!"

Corleone paused for a minute then did something that surprised the fuck out of Mac Minister. He snatched open the driver's side door of his Sunbird and said, "Bitch, get out! You gonna drive the cuddy's car!"

"What-da-fuck!" Minister exclaimed. He obviously didn't have any idea that Corleone's hoe-bitch had been sitting behind the tint watching the whole thing go down.

It didn't look like they had anything to worry about though. Danae was a trooper. After Minister and Corleone dragged Fat Tone's fat ass out the car, she hopped in with no problem. She didn't wanna know where they were heading. She just fell in line like a soldier.

I watched them leave the empty subdivision. Tone and Cowboy were left to rot in the hot Vegas sun. They didn't speed or nothing. It was a job well done. They seemed to fade from my vision until a little later when I was pulled towards a strong burst of energy located in the center of the Crest.

What the cuddies did that night ended up going down in Bay Area history. It had only been done once before and that was when we did it for The Mac.

When they got back to Vallejo, Corleone contacted all the cuddies who were real certified Country Club Crest affiliates. Romper Room niggaz who knew me since way before the music game were summoned to the turf that night. Then they had a bonfire in my memory.

The Tercel with Fat Tone's blood in the passenger seat was brought to Borges Park and set ablaze. It was a point that had to made and it was executed extremely well.

Just like the night we burned the car that belonged to the nigga who killed Mike-Mike, real gangstaz cried. They mourned the death of a real one. They poured liquor out on my behalf while telling stories of past experiences we all shared. The energy in the Crest that night was explosive, yet calming.

Then something happened... As the flames burned and dissipated the evidence so did my energy. It was as if the act of burning that car released

my energy into the cosmos.

I was set free...

Gone for eternity...

Other Books By King Guru

Guns & Roses: Book 1

Guns & Roses: Book 2

Guns & Roses: Book 3

Devils and Demons: Book 1

Devils and Demons: Book 2

Devils and Demons: Book 3

Devils and Demons: Book 4

Good Girls Love Bad Boys: An Inmate's Guide to Getting Girls

How To Hustle and Win: Sex, Money, Murder Edition

Freaky Tales

Raw Law: Your Rights and How to Sue When They are Violated

Mac Dre: The Life and Times

Psychological Seductions: Book One

Psychological Seductions: Book Two

How To Write Urban Books For Money and Fame

Underworld Zilla

Also Available

KG Magazine. The hottest non-nude exotic model magazine in the industry. Produced and published by KG Enterprise. King Guru has created a magazine that pushes the line on censors. KG Magazine is available at www.magcloud.com. Available in paper or digital form.

www.ingramcontent.com/pod-product-compliance
Lightning Source LLC
Chambersburg PA
CBHW052242220526
45471CB00001B/160